Gordon Rowley

The World Of Cristate and Variegated Succulents

Copyright © 2006 Cactus & Co.

All rights reserved. No part of this book may be reproduced in any form without written permission of the copyright owner.

Distributed to the book trade in the EU by Cactus & Co.
Alberto Marvelli via Rismondo 4, 21049 Tradate (Va) fax 0331.842921
alberto.marvelli@gmail.com

Distributed to the book trade in the USA by Rainbow Gardens Bookshop
3620 Sahuaro Divide, Tucson, Arizona 85742-9754, USA
kevin@rainbowgardensbookshop.com

ISBN-10: 88-95018-08-7
ISBN-13: 978-88-95018-08-9

Editing: Lino Di Martino

Design & Layout: Segnoruvido.comunicazioni visive
Milano 20136, via Vittadini 11
segnoruvido@segnoruvido.it

Printed in Italy by
Grafica Quadro, Tradate (VA) Italy
Digital scans & film: Eurograph, Vedano Olona (VA) Italy.

First Edition: April 2006

Cover: *Euphorbia suzannae* 'Maelstrom' (HM)

Gordon Rowley

Teratopia

The World Of Cristate and Variegated Succulents

Picture Sources

Acknowledgements and Credits

Sincere thanks are due to all who have allowed copyright material to be used in this book. Unacknowledged illustrations are the work of the author, or have been in his archive so long that the source cannot now be traced. Apologies go to anyone thus overlooked.

List of abbreviations and names

In response to a plea in the British journal (Rowley 2003) we received numerous offerings ranging from vintage slides to the latest in digital technology. To all those kind folk who responded so willingly we extend sincere thanks: their contributions add greatly to the visual and scientific appeal of the book. A mere listing of names is less then adequate reward for their generosity.

BYT	Bill & Yvonne Tree	LH	Les Hewitt
BH	Bob Humphrey	LN	Len Newton
BJ	H.A. (Bert) Jonkers		
		MC	Martin Collinson
DDL	Drude De Looze	MD	Mark Dimmitt
DS	David Scott	MS	Mark Smith
DSH	Derek Shoulders	MP	Mike Phillips
DSL	D. Slane		
DM	David Minnion	PC	P. Clayton
DT	Derek Tribble	PH	Paul Hutchison
FXS	F. X. Sammut	RND	R. N. Dehn
FDS	Francesco De Santis	RS	Robert Stephenson
GB	Geoff Bailey	SD	Rodney Sims (Pat Delaney Collection)
GC	Graham Charles	SP	Sylvia Porter
GFM	G. F. Matuszewski	SR	Stuart Riley
GR	Gordon Rowley		
GW	Graham Williamson	VG	Victor Gapon
HM	Harry Mak	WR	Werner Rauh
HB	Helmut Bannwarth	WW	William Weightman
JC	John Cox		
JH	John Hales		
JN	Joachim Noack		
JP	John Pilbeam		

Contents

7 **Preface**
9 **Introduction**
16 INTERLUDE A: Teratophilia
25 **1. Fasciation**
50 INTERLUDE B: Cristate Cacti in Habitat
63 **2. Variegation**
84 INTERLUDE C: The Colour Freak-out
91 **3. Chimeras**
105 **4. Monstrosities**
126 INTERLUDE D: Monstrosities
133 **5. Two for the price of one**
138 **6. How it all begins**
139 **7. Naming**
141 **8. Cultivation**
152 INTERLUDE E: Captive Crests
161 **9. The appeal of teratophytes**
162 INTERLUDE F: Showpieces
172 **10. Classified odds: Systematic review of teratophytes**
172 Cactaceae
204 Euphorbiaceae
218 Asclepiadaceae
224 Apocynaceae
228 Asteraceae
231 Crassulaceae
251 Agavaceae
256 Asphodelaceae
267 Aizoaceae
271 Portulacaceae
272 Passifloraceae
273 Didiereaceae
274 **11. Epilogue**
277 **Glossary**
278 **Appendix I – Recommended plants**
280 **Appendix II – Innovations**
281 **Bibliography**
284 **Index**

Fig. 1 *Melocactus intortus* in the Guadeloupe archipelago (DS)

Preface

Alice's "Curiouser and curiouser!" could not be better applied than to the subjects of this book. As if succulents were not curious enough already in their sculptural look and stark geometry, nature seems to delight in playing pranks to create strange deviants: plants with diminished symmetry or bizarre colour contrasts. Are they from this planet or from another? Some appear so different from the parent that begat them that their identity could be lost if we did not know the origin. Then one day they reveal all by throwing a reversion! The sense of wonder is not shattered, but if anything increases: evolution is going on all around us, and many are its diverse paths.

Some crests and variegates look diseased, but aren't. A few do result from infection by virus or mycoplasma, but the majority are untested and we can only guess. Some are straight mutations; others are more involved, with complicated inheritance patterns. Maltreatment of a normal plant can create dwarfs or the oddities of bonsai or topiary, but here we are concerned only with changes that have some degree of permanence and are considered horticulturally desirable.

Cristates and variegates are dismissed by some people as uniformly abominable and fit only to cast upon the dunghill (Russell 1939). Others admire the architectural beauty of well grown specimens, and welcome the extension of colouring that variegation brings to an otherwise all-green collection. Above all there is the rarity factor: they are uncompetitive in nature, and many grown in captivity are "one-offs", difficult or impossible to propagate and their unbalanced make-up demands extra care for their preservation. Nor do we have any means of creating such changes to order. They have been around in succulent collections from the start: the eye is drawn to anything novel, especially if it cloaks a mystery or challenges accepted dogma. Nurserymen were quick to seize upon them and create a connoisseur market for the choicer oddities. *Agave americana* 'Marginata' (Fig. 152) caused a sensation when it arose as a mutation and was offered for sale by a Dutch nursery for 500 Guilders in 1714. When the American Cactus & Succulent society came into being in 1929 there was already quite a vogue for cristate cacti, fronted by their first president, Dr. A.D. Houghton. His "Cactus Book" the following year devoted a whole chapter to our subject, and another to hybrids: provocative and sometimes weird, but full of personal observations and experiments. The first volume of the American

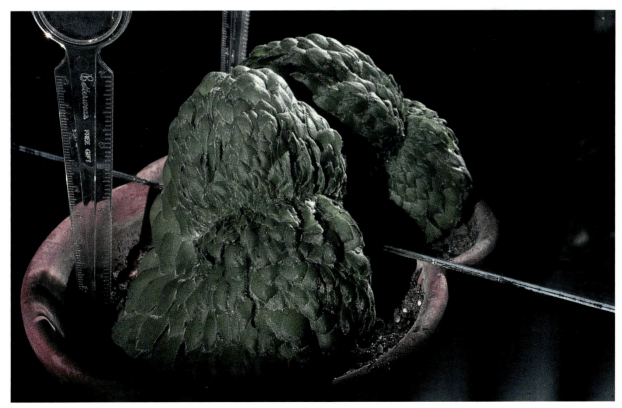

Fig. 2 *Aeonium tabuliforme* transformed from a flat rosette by fasciation. (GR)

journal invited readers to send in their experiences. A miscellany of interesting finds and pictures resulted, and it was evident that some addicts took crest-hunting seriously and organised field trips specially to hunt them out. This in turn led to reports of areas in the S.W. U.S.A. or Mexico that were especially rich in fasciations, and specialist collections of them came into being (Figs. 284, 285) in the U.S.A. and Europe. As yet I have not seen a collection entirely of variegated succulents, but on the other hand there cannot be many large collections without at least one or two.

If this book, with its copious selection of pictures, gives the impression that fasciation and variegation are common occurrences, that is certainly not true. They are never common, and in some plants and places are quite unknown. You could search a large garden for a day and not find one. Finding a good one is like winning a lottery. By analogy, imagine a future historian analysing twentieth century music-making entirely from the evidence of recordings. He could be forgiven for supposing that the commonest make of violin was the Stradivarius.

Large, well-grown specimens of cristates, such as the *Ferocactus* in Fig. 6, command instant attention, and not surprisingly are eagerly sought by collectors. Nurseries price them accordingly, although succulents do not rival orchids as playthings for the very rich, and a collection of them can be started on quite a small budget.

I hope that this first modern publication in English on cristates and variegates may further their popularity and lessen the intolerance of those who dismiss them all out of hand as a circus of disease-ridden freaks. Aside from their aesthetic merits, which must remain personal to the beholder, many of these vegetable dissidents merit preservation for their scientific interest, as yet largely unexplored.

Credits

My appeal for additional slides to supplement my own brought in a flood of spectacular pictures - too many to include them all. To all kind friends who lent their slides I owe heartfelt thanks. I hope all are correctly acknowledged (the list of credits and abbreviations is on p. 4) and will be returned safely. Especial thanks are due to Professor Lino Di Martino for the hours of work he has spent on my text through all its fasciations, variegations and monstrosities over successive typescripts. He has created another fine volume to take its place alongside those already published by Cactus & Co., all produced as a true labour of love.

Fig. 3 Variegates add colour to an all-green display and can even be subject for a collection by themselves. (HM)

Introduction

"Our most modern science is not yet able to dispense with mythical personages. A great multitude of phenomena do we attribute to Nature. Nature, even with us, is said to take all kinds of courses and make all sorts of freaks. We refer to that same old myth a thousand facts and conditions which we are still unable to explain."
—E.L. GREEN *"Landmarks of a Botanical History"* **II**: 997, 1983.

Teratology is the word coined in 1832 by Isidore Geoffroy Saint-Hilaire for the scientific study of monsters. Initially, animals attracted more attention than plants, and all manner of myths and legends grew up. A woman unfortunate enough to give birth to a malformed child was accused with having consort with the devil, and the association of disease and abnormality arose early. The occurrence of freaks and outlandish monsters has always exerted a fascination, but never more so than in the sixteenth century when it became a cult and part of the general curiosity into the divine plan of life. Collections were built up called cabinets of curiosities, the larger and more extravagant the better. Wealthy dilettantes amassed museums of giant bones, petrifactions, stuffed two-headed or deformed animals, supposed dragons and anything exotic or macabre. Among them were plant oddities: witches brooms, mandrake roots and dried fasciations. Cheating was permitted to create chimeras by stitching together bits of different animals. This is the dark side of teratology: today we are less interested in the pathology and rarity value than the light such anomalies can throw on genetics and evolution.

In the Plant Kingdom, teratology developed as a serious study in the nineteenth century, conveniently packaged in English in two publications of the Ray Society in London. *"Vegetable Teratology"* by M.T. Masters appeared in one volume in 1869, and *"Principles of Plant Teratology"* by W.C. Wordsell followed in two volumes 1915 - 1916. Both attempt a classification of plant aberrations, and both invent or adapt suitable terminology. Both attempt at great length to "explain" how freaks originate, Masters cautiously, Wordsell incautiously with anachronistic views on heredity and ontogeny. In the post-Darwinian era monsters are seen as the product of mutation, invariably at a disadvantage as compared to the norm, so that they are eliminated in the wild. Hugo De Vries, the celebrated botanist in the Netherlands at the end of the century, selected monstrosities of the evening primrose (*Oenothera*) for breeding experiments in favour of his mutation theory. Unfortunately what he didn't know was that the greatest monstrosity in *Oenothera* lies in its chromosomes, united in rings and inherited as such, which upset his breeding ratios and led to the sudden appearance of new major deviants in the progenies. "Monsters", renamed "Macro-mutations" became involved in the conflict among evolutionists on whether evolution progressed by small stages or by abrupt leaps.

Human attitudes to them vary, as does the definition of what we call monstrose. We are repelled at the sight of deformed animals, yet cherish highly bred dogs, birds and fish, unlike anything in nature and wholly dependent upon us for survival. The most esteemed roses of our garden are monsters, bred from four or more wild species and often almost or completely sterile. Fortunately the aesthetics of teratology need not concern us here, although the issue of how they come about has to be faced, if only because it is the first question any observer asks: "How did my plant come to do this?" Perhaps the best answer to that would be: "I don't know, I wasn't there when it happened!" The subject will be addressed more formally in the chapter on fasciation, along with the equally tantalising "how can you make plants go cristate?"

Of the numerous types of teratological growth in plants, two are of major interest here, and both are exceptionally well represented in the plants we call succulent. The first is **fasciation**, a fairly well-defined phenomenon that turns a normally cylindrical stem into a wedge, fan or **crest**, that later may become convoluted into a brain-like mass (see Figs. 4-8). This involves a change in symmetry from radial to bilateral: the stem ceases to grow in length, but instead grows sideways in one plane. This may lead to a specimen very unlike the normal parent, with smaller leaves, more ribs, altered branching and suppression of flowers. Some **cristate** plants remain tiny gems; others expand well beyond the proportions of unfasciated plants: a *Ferocactus* over 1 m wide (Snyder & Weber 1966), or the saguaro, *Carnegiea*, over 4 m from tip to tip.

Second is **variegation**, the partial absence of chlorophyll, the green pigment contained in lens-shaped plastids within the cells and essential for photosynthesis to take place. Its localised

Fig. 4 Cristate cacti grafted on tall cerei in the nursery of Horst Uebelmann in Germany. (GR)

Fig. 5 (Above) Probably the most massive crests in succulents are those on the giant saguaro, *Carniegea gigantea*. This one flourishes in the Sonora Desert Museum, Arizona. (GR)

Fig. 6 (Right) Large crested *Ferocactus wislizeni* in a nursery in Demig, New Mexico. (GR)

Introduction

Fig. 7 *Copiapoa cinerea* ssp. *haseltoniana* (*gigantea*) crest, in habitat in Chile (GC)

Fig. 8 *Mammillaria elongata* crest. All the pleats and folds arise from a single root. (HM)

absence leads to leaves or stems having stripes or blotches of yellow or white (or orange or purple if other pigments are present). Total absence gives an albino plant, that can survive only parasitically as a graft on a green stock. Variegation is an essentially different phenomenon from fasciation, involving the side-by-side development of two cell lineages, one producing normal green chlorophyll, the other non-green. We call such a plant combining two or more genetically distinct tissues a **chimera** after the legendary monster made up of bits of different animals joined together.

Fig. 9 (Above) *Pachypodium lamerei* 'Particolour' is marbled with yellow each spring, but goes almost entirely green as the season advances. (GR)

Fig. 10 (Left) *Acanthocalycium spiniflorum (violaceum)* variegated; a mericlinal chimera. (HM)

Introduction

Fig. 11 *Echinopsis eyriesii* variegated. (HM)

Fig. 12 (Above) *Senecio kleinia* 'Candystick' shows a different colour scheme from the usual green and yellow. (GR)

Fig. 13 (Left) Variegation in *Opuntia* (rear left), *Mammillaria* (rear right), *Gymnocalycium* (front left) and *Portulacaria* (front right). Without chlorophyll, the mammillaria is sustained by a green stock. (GR)

Observant plantsmen often encounter teratologies among their charges, when nature's not-quite-infallible programming seems to slip a cog: oddly shaped leaves, freakish flowers, twinned fruits and so on. Most are "one-off" events, perhaps resulting from some sort of injury, and unlikely to excite the collecting urge. **Double flowers**, with stamens and sometimes carpels replaced by petal-like organs, are one exception, but outside the present survey. Very few succulents qualify.

Monstrosities in the narrow sense are plants resembling fasciations but with even greater loss of symmetry, and lacking a single dominant, linear apex (Fig. 14). The adjective **monstrose** is preferable to monstrous which implies malignancy. **Proliferation** is a different phenomenon in which every bud that can grow does, giving a

Fig. 14 Most sculptural of all cactus monsters is monolithic *Pachycereus* (*Lophocereus*) *schottii* 'Monstrosus', and it occurs in the wild. (GR)

cauliflower-like appearance to the plant (Fig. 15). Other aberrations include **spiral torsion**, **spinelessness** (Fig. 16) and **foliar follies**: appendages emerging from leaves.

Teratology seems to be a no-man's land for research, combining as it does aspects of morphology, genetics and pathology but shunned by investigators of all three disciplines. Hence there is a dearth of general literature. Among succulents, the one and only book is *"The Enigma of the Origin of Monstrosity and Cristation in Succulent Plants"* by J.J.V. Wolthuys that came out in Dutch and English in 1938 and was reprinted in a revised form in 1948. This is an admirable introduction to the subject for growers, but as the title suggests gives so much prominence to the unanswerable question that it seems to have discouraged future inquiries. However, the periodicals on gardening and succulents teem with isolated illustrations and notes on freaks and oddities, and a hunt down the highways and byways of scientific journals brings to light enough evidence to show that, if we are still uncertain about the initial stages, the early development and elaboration from aberrant meristems are well understood and provide an appropriate introduction to their subsequent expansion and diversification. As regards terminology, despite a wealth of technical terms, mostly rare or long forgotten, to cover different types of aberration, I have yet to see **teratophyte** for any teratological plant, which seems a useful addition to the language, along with **teratophile** and **teratophobe** for the person who respectively loves or hates such oddities.

This book presents a picture gallery of succulent teratophytes selected for their beauty, rarity or desirability for collections. There can be no completeness, no systematic catalogue or identification key: novelties are arising all the time, and when least expected. Formal descriptions, on the lines of those in floras and monographs, would serve little purpose. More to the point are details of availability, propagation and cultural treatment. Overall the pictures give a cross-section of what is to be seen in the wild and in captivity, and as such they may serve to stimulate new converts to take up a challenging, unpredictable but hugely rewarding study.

Introduction

Fig. 15 *Disocactus* (*Aporocactus*) *mallisonii* 'Monstrosus' attempts to grow from every areole. (GR)

Fig. 16 A spineless *Mammillaria* seedling, one of many such mutants that turn up from time to time where cacti are raised from seed by the thousand. (GR)

Fig. 17 Some species are more prone to teratological lapses than others. *Pachypodium lamerei* produces crests and variegates in diversity. (GR)

Interlude A
Teratophilia

This book aims to present teratophytes to as wide an audience as possible: not only horticulturists and botanists, but also to artists and designers for the three-dimensional sculptural appeal of the plants, their texture and extraordinary coloration. To this end the text has been kept to a minimum, and the chapters are interwoven between pictorial interludes further illustrating the subject matter on either side.

The first such intermission concentrates on plants in cultivation, some common and easy-growing, such as the *Sempervivum* in Fig. 30 and *Haworthia* 'Harry Mak' in Fig. 34; others rare or exceptionally well-grown specimens that qualify for the show bench.

Those with branches or offsests could be split up and propagated.

Solitary heads like the *Melocactus* in Fig. 18 could not, and one would have to search thousands of seedlings in hope of finding another to match. The non-green *Haworthia truncata* in Fig. 32 could probably not last long detached from the normal green rosette in the background that supplies it with food.

Teratophilia

Fig. 18 (Above) showing monstrose growth of *Copiapoa tenuissima* affecting the development of spines and hairs. (HM)

Fig. 19 (Left) A rare variegated *Melocactus*. (HM)

Fig. 20 (Below) A *Frailea* showing repeated fasciation on every head - an indication that the cause is genetical rather than environmental. (HM)

Teratophilia

Opposite page:

Fig. 21 (Above) A *Parodia* showing a combination of fasciation, spine suppression and disordered growth. (HM)

Fig. 22 (Below) *Lophophora williamsii* crest: a remarkably fine specimen. (SR)

This page:

Fig. 23 (Above) This *Sulcorebutia rauschii*, alias *Rebutia canigueralii*, cristate was grown from de Herdt seed. (LH)

Fig. 24 (Middle) *Echinopsis* 'Johnson's Gold', a remarkable "peanut cactus" that sports particoloured flowers. (GR)

Fig. 25 (Below) *Pilosocereus pachycladus* (*azureus*), a phalangial cristate. (SD)

Fig. 26 (Upper left) *Mammillaria gracilis* 'Bunty', a popular mutant cultivar. (HM)

Fig. 27 (Middle left) *Cleistocactus parapetiensis* cristate flourishing on its own roots. (GR)

Fig. 28 (Lower left) *Aeonium* 'Spreading Sun'. (HM)

Teratophilia

Fig. 29 (Upper right) *Monilaria moniliformis* cristate, a very rare example of fasciation in the Aizoaceae (mesembs). (GR)

Fig. 30 (Middle right) *Sempervivum calcareum* 'Grigg's Surprise', frost hardy and known to have reverted to type, so possibly a chimera. (HM)

Fig. 31 (Lower right) *Gasteria nitida* var. *armstrongii* 'Yellow Cow', a striking mericlinal chimera from Harry Mak. (SD)

Fig. 32 (Above) *Haworthia truncata* sporting an offset apparently lacking chlorophyll. (HM)

Fig. 33 (Left) *Gasteria* cv. (variegated). Many striking teratophytes, such as this striped *Gasteria*, arise from chance or hybrid seed and are so bizarre that their parentage cannot be assessed. (HM)

Teratophilia

Fig. 34 (Above) *Haworthia cymbiformis* 'Harry Mak', officially named here after the enthusiastic collector and distributor of succulent cultivars, is a widely grown and vigorous cultivar that sports variegated, pallid and all-green rosettes from one root. The last are best removed to encourage more variegation. It is the ideal beginner's introduction to variegated leaf succulents. (HM)

Fig. 35 (Right) *Haworthia limifolia* 'Stripes'. (HM)

Fig. 36 (Left)
Crassula orbicularis, spiral torsion. (GR)

Fig. 37 (Below)
This clone of *Euphorbia milii* 'Golden Crown' is strikingly colourful, but lacks the stamina of the normal "crown of thorns". (GR)

Fasciation
chapter 1

First things first

The lowliest forms of plantlife, such as algae, grow from a single apical cell that by repeated division forms a chain which may then divide in line with the axis to form a thicker cylinder or flat strap. It was indeed a great step forward for plantkind when the multicellular **meristem** evolved, programmed to differentiate the expanding mass of cells to form distinct tissues with different roles to play within the plant. All the higher plants are thus endowed. We know that early on in the differentiation of a seedling a mechanism comes into play determining a left and right polarity in the stem. This is shown by the disposition of cotyledons: two, in the case of dicotyledons, sited exactly opposite to one another. This is significant, because it helps us understand one of the basic characteristics of fasciation: growth to left and right rather than all round or in a spiral. We can call such fanlike expansions **bilateral** (Fig. 38). Rarely, only one side goes on expanding (as in *Crassula muscosa* Fig. 220 or *Pachypodium lamerei* Fig. 39) giving a cockscomb or **unilateral** crest.

Here we look only at the stems of succulents. These are generally fatter than those of other plants and have accordingly wider meristems: about 0.7 mm wide in *Echinocereus reichenbachii* shown in Fig. 40). Here we see a vertical section through the tip of the cactus stem, with the "mountain range" on the left representing the birth of successive areoles along a rib, and a gap between two ribs on the right. An epidermis one cell thick covers the whole. The meristem cells continue dividing, and further back down the stem we can recognise different lineages of cells associated with different functions: food storage, transport, mechanical support, and so on. It is all very impressive; so highly organised, so quietly efficient and so utterly reliable and repeatable from one aeon to the next. Yet malfunctions do occur, albeit very rarely, and it is those malfunctions that concern us here.

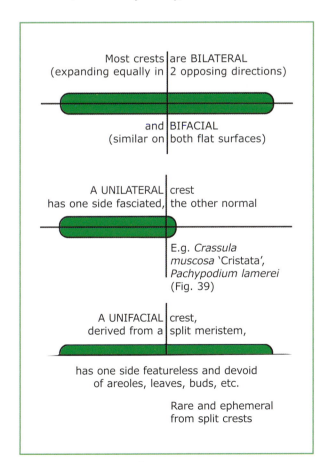

Fig. 38 Symmetry and Cristation

Fig. 39 *Pachypodium lamerei*: unilateral crest. (GR)

Looked at from above, a normal cactus meristem is represented in simplified form in Fig. 42A (p. 26). The six radial lines of bumps represent the six ribs of an *Echinocereus*. When branching takes place, it does so from one of the lateral areoles, through which a new meristem emerges. The remaining diagrams show the products of abnormal meristem activity. In Fig. 42B it has divided into two equal halves (**dichotomy**). This is a rare occurrence in flowering plants, but has become the norm in just a few fat-stemmed mam-

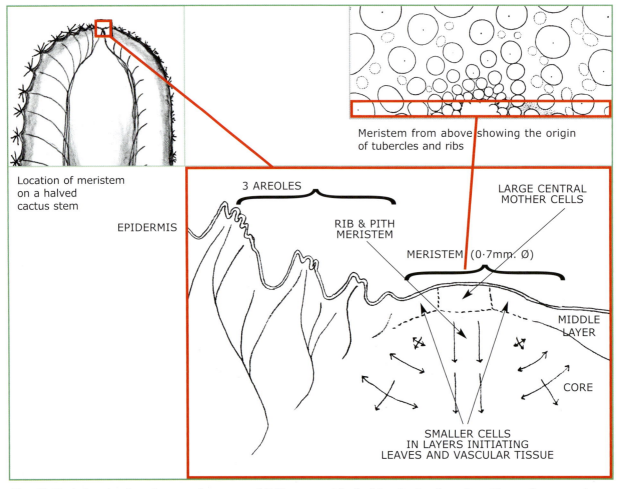

Fig. 40 Vertical section through a normal stem apex of *Echinocereus reichenbachii* and a view from above. The smaller arrows show the directions of cell expansion. (After Boke 1951)

Fig. 41 Splitting of one head into two (dichotomy) is the normal mode of branching in *Mammillaria perbella* and a few related species. (GR)

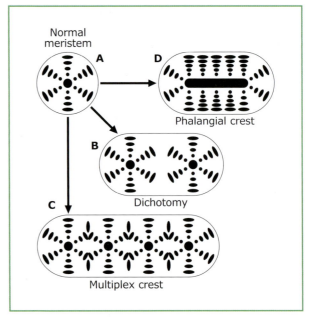

Fig. 42 Types of crests

Fasciation

Fig. 43 *Echinocactus ingens* stem apex widening with age. (GR)

millarias (Fig. 41; Boke 1976, p. 26). It also occurs in *Euphorbia multiclava* and *E. piscidermis* (Rauh 1988). It will not be mentioned further here, and is included only to put it in context with other growth aberrations.

In Fig. 42C the initial dichotomy has repeated, and by continuing to do so produced an ever-extending row of daughter meristems packed together so closely that they expand as a single wedge- or fan-shaped (flabellate) crest. This I call a **multiplex** (or "many folds") crest, a term also used to describe double flowers like a garden rose with many tightly crowded petals.

The most extreme type of fasciation is represented in Fig. 42D. Here a single meristem has expanded in two directions (bilaterally) to form a line leading to a ribbon or wedge-like growth as in the previous example. **Phalangial** is the best adjective I can find to describe this sort of crest, comparing it to a phalanx or line of soldiers advancing as one man. Others would see a parallel to a widening river or its delta.

Fig. 44 *Mammillaria muehlenpfordtii* showing a widening of the stem apex, common in large old plants. (GR)

The difference between multiplex and phalangial crests needs a powerful lens or microscope to detect and I would not recommend it as a basis for classification, especially as some plants have been shown to produce both types. In succulents, a multiplex apex was first shown in *Orbea variegata* by Jonsson & Gorenflot in 1969 and 1970 (Fig. 48, p. 29), and a phalangial apex in *Echinocereus reichenbachii* by Boke & Ross in 1978 (Fig. 49). Long ridge-like crests that go into brain-like contortions without throwing normal shoots, such as *Pachypodium lamerei* 'Curlycrest' (Fig. 47, p. 28) can be assumed to be phalangial; those that frequently revert, as for example *Senecio serpens* 'Albert Baynes' (Fig. 46, p. 28) are probably multiplex. In both types, if the apex is damaged or removed, lateral branches can be expected to grow normally, at least initially, without cristation.

Fig. 45 *Epithelantha micromeris* trifid apex. Such di- and trichotomies are stable and rarely go on to become fully fasciated. (GR)

Fig. 46 *Senecio serpens* 'Albert Baynes', a multiplex cristate, is worth preserving by cutting off any shoots that revert to normal. (GR)

Fig. 47 *Pachypodium lamerei* 'Curlycrest' forming a single ever-widening phalangial crest thrown into irregular folds and pleats. (GR)

Fasciation

Fig. 48 Multiplex crest of *Orbea variegata* (After Jonsson 1970). Note the opposite, decussate phyllotaxy of the stem apices.

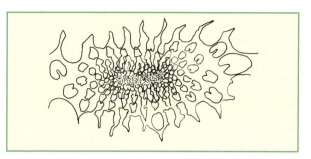

Fig. 49 Phalangial crest of *Echinocereus reichenbachii* (After Boke & Ross 1978). Both are viewed from above.

When fasciation takes over, a stem stops elongating and increases in width. Crests rarely grow longer, except by reversion or sprouting new crests. What is harder to conceive is why they widen in one plane only. This is the key distinction from monstrose growth which shows a further reduction in symmetry and branching at random. Clearly there are many genes controlling shoot architecture, and we are witness to different types of malfunction.

Fasciation changes the symmetry from radial to bilateral, but in other respects little else changes. Cut across the short axis, the crest looks no different from an ordinary stem, as seen in Fig. 42. Such changes as occur can be related to problems of space and nutrition. Leaves may become more numerous and smaller, the axis may remain shorter than normal, and flowering may never be possible. In terms of survival in the wild, most of these changes are for the worse. But some spontaneously occurring cristate and monstrose succulents look surprisingly healthy and outgrow the normal plant in bulk and dimensions (Fig. 50). In cultivation, I find that the cristate clone grown from side branches of *Euphorbia woodii* 'Salad Bowl' (Fig. 51) is faster growing and less temperamental than the "medusa head" original: it is as if the expanded frond-like shoots were better adapted to mild temperate conditions than the highly xeromorphic original.

Mention of *Euphorbia woodii* (Fig. 52) introduces certain succulents for which more than one fasciated form exists. Fig. 53 shows a "head crest" of the same species, where the branches are normal but the main axis alone is fasciated. In *Melocactus* the main

Fig. 50 *Pachycereus* (*Lophocereus*) *schottii* 'Monstrosus' in the Desert Botanic Garden in Arizona. (GR)

Fig. 51 *E. woodii* 'Salad Bowl' grown from a crested side branch, with no development of a main trunk. (GR)

Fig. 52 *Euphorbia woodii* (*flanaganii*) has a stout caudex-like main stem and many spirally set thin branches, the "Medusa head spurge". Either can become fasciated. (GR)

Fig. 53 *E. woodii* 'Bighead Medusa' with the main axis fasciated and the side branches as normal. (GR)

Fasciation

Fig. 54 *Echeveria* 'Ramiletta' benefits from breaking up and starting afresh from time to time, incidentally supplying duplicates for exchange. (GR)

Fig. 55 *Echeveria setosa* 'Candy Floss' in various stages of reversion to normal rosettes. (GR)

axis or the inflorescence (cephalium) can fasciate (Figs. 67–69), producing strikingly dissimilar results.

The subsequent development of a crest from a simple wedge is shown in Fig. 58. Continued growth in one plane inevitably leads to space problems, resulting in undulations and eventually a brainlike mass if by now reversion to normal shoots has not occurred (Figs. 56, 57). The phenomenon of an indefinitely broadening meristem is unique to phalangial crests; just how wide it can eventually become one can only guess. With the aid of a ball of string I once measured the twists and turns of the ridge on a large *Pachypodium* 'Curlycrest': just over 4.5 m, and a world record until somebody measures a

Fig. 56 *Opuntia cylindrica* 'Cristata', easy on its own roots and a good choice for the beginner's collection. (GR)

Fig. 57 *Mammillaria spinosissima* 'Cristata'. Fine show specimens like this take many years to mature but are not more difficult than the typical species to grow. (GR)

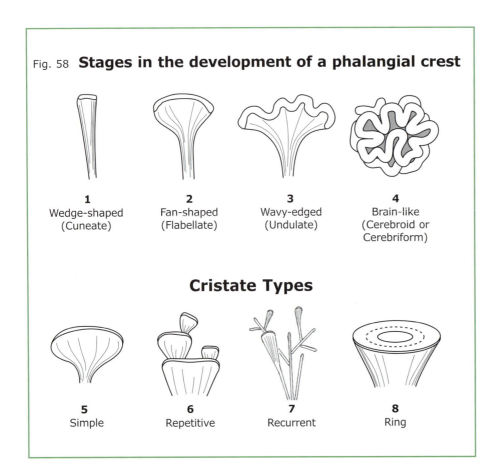

Fig. 58 **Stages in the development of a phalangial crest**

1 Wedge-shaped (Cuneate)
2 Fan-shaped (Flabellate)
3 Wavy-edged (Undulate)
4 Brain-like (Cerebroid or Cerebriform)

Cristate Types

5 Simple
6 Repetitive
7 Recurrent
8 Ring

Examples

1. *Adenia globosa*
2 *Bergerocactus emoryi*
3 *Echinopsis chamaecereus*
4 *Lobivia haematantha*
5 *Euphorbia piscidermis*
6 *Opuntia subulata* var. *exaltata*
7 *Pedilanthus macrocarpus*
8 *Melocactus broadwayi*

larger one! Every centimetre of this is an active phalangial meristem, and if cut out and grafted would reproduce the phenomenon.

Early theorists - Linnaeus among them - regarded fasciation as the fusion of many shoots into one ("*fascis*" is a bundle, packet or sheaf). This definition is explicit or implied in just about every dictionary, botanical or otherwise, that I have consulted, and nobody has yet pointed out to the compilers that it is the very opposite of what actually takes place. There is no fusion of adjacent parts in fasciation, no confluence of self-grafting. Instead we have an originally single apex expanding like a stream widening into a river or a trickle of sand becoming a delta.

Ring cristates

One special type of cristation deserves attention: the ring cristate, in which the phalangial ridge forms a complete circle around a "neutral" centre, and growth takes place rather like inflating a tyre inner tube. Knox (1908) studied ring fasciations in the evening primrose (*Oenothera*) and her serial sections of stem tips show how a normal meristem expands into a ring and duplicates the same vascular system and external tissues internally as on the outside. Simple, when you know how! Eventually the ring may split down one side and flatten out, completing the overall anatomy of a normal stem, but elliptical instead of circular. The best cactus example I have seen is a specimen of *Echinopsis* (*Lobivia*) *haematantha* given me many years ago as a seedling (Rowley 1984, 1993; Fig.

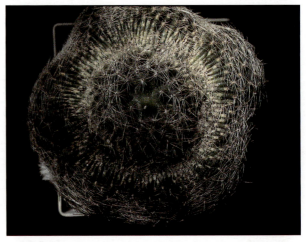

Fig. 59 Ring cristate *Echinopsis* (*Lobivia*) *haematantha* ssp. *densispina*. Note the "neutral" centre encircled by the meristem. (GR)

Fasciation

59). The normal plant forms heads 7–8 cm in diameter. The ring cristate expanded into an inverted cone 12 cm tall and 9 cm across, with a sunken centre lacking areoles. Subsequently the funnel-like shape was lost as the pressure of new growth threw it into weird contortions and lumps (Fig. 60). Initial flowers were normal, but then further surprises were added as cristate blooms extruded from the ridge (see below). Unfortunately there is no way that ring cristates of this type can be propagated to retain their unique form.

Two succulents are outstanding for routinely producing a percentage of ring-cristate growths, depending on how vigorously they are grown: *Orbea* (*Diplocyatha*) *ciliata* (Fig. 65) and *Opuntia clavarioides* (Fig. 66, p. 34). In the clones most commonly found in cultivation, normal stems are club-shaped, but are usually accompanied by some that are larger, funnel-shaped and with a depressed inert centre. In the opuntia the shape is more variable and the top often elevated into five or more fingerlike brown outgrowths, giving rise to an apt but, regrettably, highly politically incorrect cultivar name, for which I have heard no innocent replacement. The origin of these is uncertain, and it is on record that the opuntia shows equal variation in the wild.

Fig. 60 The same plant later: the ring has been thrown into irregular folds, and two normal flowers arise from lateral areoles. (GR)

Fig. 61 The same plant with a cristate flower (left) arising direct from the phalangial meristem, and a normal flower (right). (GR)

Fig. 62 Interior of the cristate flower showing 98 stigmas – nearly ten times the number for one normal flower. (GR)

Fig. 63 (Above left) *Rebutia heliosa*: a fine example of a ring cristate on one branch. (DSL)

Fig. 64 (Above right) *Gymnocalycium mucidum* showing ring cristation. (DT)

Fig. 65 (Left) *Orbea (Diplocyatha) ciliata* is treasured by stapeliad lovers for its remarkable blooms. Plants in cultivation throw up curious ring-cristate shoots like the one on the right. (GR)

Fig. 66 (Below Left) *Opuntia clavarioides* grows club-shaped joints but also occasional larger ring-cristate mushroom-like shoots (top left) sometimes with finger-like outgrowths on top. (GR)

Fasciation

Figs. 67 (above), **68, 69** (below) *Melocactus broadwayi* in Curaçao: a unique ring-cristate specimen found and photographed by Mark Smith. Note the lifebuoy-shaped cephalium. (MS)

Fasciated roots and leaves

Thus far attention has been confined to fasciation in stems, but other parts of a plant grow from meristems that are also liable to freak out. Fasciated roots occur probably more often than we know, because they are hidden below soil and when revealed do not excite the finder to paeans of praise (Figs. 71, 545). An example of cristate roots originating from a cutting of *Mammillaria microcarpa* is illustrated in Saguaroland Bulletin 16: 102, 1962, amusingly captioned "a fascinated root". For fasciated leaves the ferns have a near-monopoly, if one counts those cultivars with strangely quilled and frilled fronds like parsley that were the delight of shady Victorian conservatories. A single example in succulents comes from the most highly reduced stemless mesembs, where *Lithops* has come up with neat examples of up to nine leaf lobes in place of the normal two (Fig. 70).

Fig. 70 *Lithops pseudotruncatella* crest with 8 leaf lobes in place of the normal 2 from a multiplex meristem. (GR)

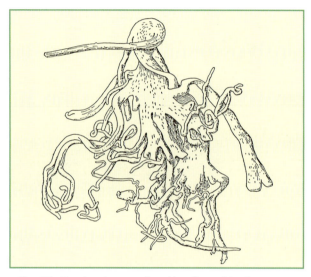

Fig. 71 Fasciated roots of an *Aloe*, figured in the Gardener's Chronicle for 1900.

Fasciated flowers and fruits

The leaf-cristate lithops shown in Fig. 70 went on to produce a fasciated flower (Fig. 72) followed by a giant capsule full of seeds, apparently from self-pollination. However, none of the seedlings raised from it showed more than two cotyledons or any subsequent sign of fasciation, and the parent plant itself reverted to normal over a period of years (Rowley 1985a).

Many cristates never manage to flower, or only after reversion to normal growth. Others flower normally from buds below the crest. Multiplex crests may throw up buds and flowers which are no different from those on non-fasciated plants (Fig.73). Phalangial crests offer the best hope for fasciated flowers, but on the other hand one sometimes encounters a cristate flower arising from an apparently quite normal plant. An outstanding example of this is a clone of *Rebutia steinbachii* (*Sulcorebutia oenantha*) that regularly produces fan-shaped flowers, al-

Fig. 72 The same *Lithops* with a normal flower (right) and a cristate flower (left). (GR)

Fasciation

Fig. 73 A fasciated *Echinopsis* throwing up normal flowers from lateral areoles. (GR)

Fig. 74 *Gymnocalycium mihanovichii* 'Tegelberg's Beauty' producing normal flowers (left) and cristate ones (right) from a multiplex meristem. (DSH)

though the plant body is completely normal: an interesting mutant considering the elongated areole of sulcorebutias. Twin ovaries joined like a figure 8 are not uncommon as a first stage to fasciation. In extreme cases like the flowers of *Echinopsis* shown on p. 33 one can count the number of styles as a rough guide to compare with those in a normal flower: the equivalent of ten blooms in this case.

Fasciated fruits also occur. I recall my early childhood encounter with double and multiplex bananas eagerly sought among the bunches on the greengrocer's stall. But it would be a lot to expect fasciated seeds – and I am not forgetting the largest of all, the "double coconut" *Lodoicea*.

Fig. 75 *Ferocactus wislizeni* cristate with normal yellow fruits. (JH)

Occurrence of fasciation in the Plant Kingdom

Cristation is unrecorded in some groups of vascular plants. I have seen no example in cycads or ferns, although the extravagantly frilled and crisped leaves of some fern cultivars seem to qualify as leaf fasciation. Fasciation is more or less confined to the higher realms of vascular plants, but is not evenly distributed throughout the flowering plants (Angiosperms). As it involves a change in growth organisation at the stem tip, anatomical features here seem to be relevant. Thin woody stems of trees and shrubs rarely fasciate, and then usually only to form a narrow multiplex wedge that aborts or soon reverts to normal shoots. But there are exceptions. Indeed, one claimant to have grown the largest of all crests is a conifer, an Australian species of *Araucaria*.

Broad, soft stems fasciate more readily than narrow woody ones, and they don't come broader or fleshier than in the succulents. Xerophytes seem prone to go cristate; aquatics, marsh plants and epiphytes do not. The frequency of fasciation in succulents varies from Family to Family. Here we must recognise the distinction between the two great groups that make up flowering plants, the Monocotyledons and the Dicotyledons. Nowadays increasing evidence supports the distinction and suggests that divergence occurred at a very early stage in evolution.

Around nine-tenths of all known succulents fall within the dicots. These have an opposite pair of cotyledons (seed leaves) and simple or divided, often stalked leaves (when present) with netlike venation. There are other features, but the one that concerns us especially here is what happens to perennials when they develop secondary wood. Their conducting (vascular) system is arranged in a circle with a pith in the centre, and in shrubs and trees wood develops concentrically to form the familiar type of tree trunk that can be dated by counting the rings. The smaller group of monocots includes the palms, lilies, grasses and orchids. Succulence has evolved in *Aloe* and *Agave* and related genera, and in a few oddities like yams (*Dioscorea*) and bulbs (*Bowiea*). These all germinate with a single cotyledon, and typically have simple, elongated, stalkless leaves with parallel veins (*Dioscorea* excepted). The vascular bundles are scattered throughout the stem and not adapted to form rings of secondary wood. Where tree status is achieved, as in palms, some aloes, yuccas and dracaenas, the result looks very different from forest trees: a simple stem with usually few or no branches and supported by interwoven fibres, which form a complete sheath in palms. We can relate these anatomical differences to differences in fasciation frequency and variegation patterns in the following table.

Fig. 76 A rare example of cristation in monocots: a fasciated *Haworthia*. (SD)

Fasciation

	MONOCOTYLEDONS	**DICOTYLEDONS**
Succulent representatives	Agavaceae s. lat. (*Agave, Sansevieria*, etc.) *Liliaceae* s.lat. (*Aloe, Haworthia, Gasteria, Bulbine, Bowiea*, etc.) Dioscoreaceae (*Dioscorea* in part) Also quasi-succulent Bromeliaceae, Orchidaceae	All remaining succulents
Stem anatomy	Vascular bundles scattered; no secondary wood.	Vascular bundles in 1 or more concentric rings; often woody.
Fasciation	Very rare	**Herbaceous:** Common, especially in broad-tipped fleshy stems; often irreversible. **Woody:** Uncommon; mostly wedge-shaped and unstable.
Grafting	Rarely practicable	Potentially all possible
Leaves	Narrow, with parallel veining	Mostly broad, net-veined
Variegation	Stripes, streaks or cross-bands	Marginal, blotches, mottles, dots

Reversion

Reference has already been made to the tendency for some cristates to throw normal shoots, or even to grow out into a line of wholly normal stems, nicely shown in one of the earliest illustrations of fasciated succulents, a *Huernia reticulata* plate by Jacquin, published around 1806 (Fig. 77, p. 40). In cultivation, we find a complete range of behavioural patterns. Some never revert. These are mostly dwarf stem succulents that produce a single fan and no flowers, and remain unique unless one is bold enough to cut wedges out of the (phalangial) ridge and root or graft them. Others revert only when old or starved (Fig. 78, p. 40). Typically, a new cristate goes through a predictable life-cycle, beginning with a great burst of activity requiring generous feeding to expand profligate growth into its grandest proportions. Some people believe that overfeeding alone is enough to trigger off cristate-prone species into performing. Eventually, overcrowding or lessening resources causes growth to slow down, and it is then that a return to normal shoots may occur. Wise cultivators recognise that a prized cristate, more than a normal plant, remains at its peak for only a limited period, and take steps to propagate it in case the decline happens too rapidly (i.e. the day before the show, or when visitors are expected).

Fig. 77 *Huernia reticulata*, Plate 9 of Jacquin's folio of Stapeliae, Part I, published around 1806, showing how a fan-like multiplex crest has completely reverted to normal shoots.

Fig. 78 *Pygmaeocereus bylesianus* (*rowleyanus*): an ancient cristate that has started to revert to normal heads. (GR)

Some cristates revert so easily that it is a continual struggle to keep them pruned and maintain at least one viable crest. Many are lost before they ever enter the horticultural circuit. The more desirable the cristate, the greater the efforts to preserve it, and some notoriously unstable cultivars have been around for many decades: *Senecio serpens* 'Albert Baynes' (Fig. 46, p. 28) and several crested echeverias and aeoniums. Frequent reversion can, however, be a blessing in disguise. My cristate *Echeveria setosa* (Fig. 55, p. 31) is a never-ending source of normal rosettes for summer bedding or exchange, and reversions from the less stable crests of *Pachypodium lamerei* (Fig. 47, p. 28) can be rooted up as stocks for grafting.

Induced fasciation

Many attempts have been made to induce plants to go cristate, spurred on by the high value put upon specimens by specialist collectors. Some were undertaken following the observation that plants were fasciating following freak weather or environmental hazards. Those who were around when systemic weedkillers were first introduced may recall that they were sprayed with careless abandon on hedgerows and most dandelions (*Taraxacum*) came up more or less fasciated. A more shocking example followed the Chernobyl atomic disaster in which plants in the landscape were seen to be grotesquely contorted as if fasciated. People attributed fasciation to the effects of hailstones, lightning, earthquakes, mechanical injury from grazing, soil toxins and much else. Wolthuys (1948) adds to the list, with innocent succulents subjected to every imaginable form of torture from crushing, cutting, acupuncture, poison injections, over- or under-feeding and drought to treatment with hormones, irradiation and mutagens to upset chromosome make-up. A convincing case for insect damage as triggering off fasciation in the highly fasciation-prone genus *Oenothera* (evening primrose) was made by Alice Knox in 1908. The predators minutely punctured the tip of the meristem in their feeding; attempts to imitate the damage with even the finest surgical needle merely killed the cells. She also found that the extent of fasciation was dependent on nutrition: the better the plants were fed, the more extravagant the crest formation. The net result of all these experiments, at least so far as succulents are concerned, is discouraging. Species already known to be prone to fasciate sometimes obliged; others formed monstrose growth but, if they survived, eventually grew out normally. I do not know of any cultivar on offer today that was created to order in this way - even from Japan.

Infective Fasciation

One commonly hears fasciated plants spoken of dismissively as diseased, and some people even worry that their other plants might become infected. So is there any truth in the slight? Little or none, so far as we know, because so few succulents have been subjected to proper examination. The test of a virus is that it can pass across a graft union, and this will be seen later to be true for a few tested cases of variegation and proliferation. As far back as 1920 it was discovered that a normal grapevine grafted on to a fasciation-prone vine stock would itself become cristate (White 1948: 348). Could this also be true of some succulents? We urgently need some experimentation here before even making guesses as to the answer.

One teratological phenomenon that is certainly pathological is proliferation, a quite different growth change from fasciation although it has unfortunately been confused with that by some researchers. The subject is covered later in the chapter on miscellaneous monstrosities (p. 111).

Initiation and Inheritance

The most plausible explanation put forward to account for the spontaneous appearance of fasciation invokes not one but two factors, one genetical, the other environmental. Ability to fasciate may well be programmed into the DNA for most (or all?) higher plants, but it requires a stimulus of some sort to trigger it into action. In this respect fasciation is comparable to flowering, or to change from a juvenile to an adult life form. In the previous section on induced fasciation numerous factors were mentioned that might or might not induce cristation in a susceptible plant. But the triggering could equally come from within at the level of genes and chromosomes.

In a fasciation-prone plant, initiation can take place at different stages in the life cycle:
I. The seedling is cristate from the start, and remains so throughout its lifetime.
II. The seedling appears normal but its main axis later fasciates so that all subsequent growth is as a crest (Fig. 79, below).
III. The whole plant appears normal until one or more branch tips fasciate (Fig. 80, p. 42).

It can be assumed that propagation from any part other than the crest will grow on as normal, unless the process repeats itself at some time in the future. In this respect it is interesting to quote the case of a *Huernia pillansii* in the collection of Mrs. Vera Higgins (renowned for her disapproval of "monsters") as reported in Wolthuys 1948: 53. Her plant slipped from favour so far as to produce a single cristate shoot, which she promptly cut off. However, the performance was repeated four times

Fig. 79 The "fish-scale spurge", *Euphorbia piscidermis*, shows an endearing tendency to fasciate in cultivation. Here a seedling has grown normally for some years and suddenly become swollen-headed. (GR)

Fig. 80 An old clump of *Mammillaria geminispina* has sported a single cristate head. This could be cut off and propagated. (GR)

over the same place on the plant. This may not prove four mutations; the new sprouts might have come from the same multiplex meristem below.

Once the plant has become cristate, we need to consider how far its progeny, if any, will turn into crests. Many crests never bloom, no matter how large or old they become or how much one coaxes them with water, fertiliser and a sun-ray lamp. In terms of seed and progeny, it makes no difference if the flowers are normal or themselves cristate. Most commonly, no seedlings fasciate, or only a very few. We can summarise cristate behaviour patterns in the table below.

Examples of all five types are found throughout higher plants, and succulents are no exception. In Type V plants, fasciation is inherited, obeys Mendelian laws of segregation and recombination, and manifests from the start without an obvious external stimulus being needed. A single recessive gene may be responsible, but generally modifier genes are involved too, giving complex ratios and degrees of expression.

A Cristates barren or non-flowering (or untested as yet)	
B Unpropagatable "one-offs"; non-revertible	I
BB Propagatable vegetatively by cuttings or grafts	
C Non-revertible	II
CC Revertible	III
AA Cristates fertile and seed-setting	
D Not true-breeding, or breeding as normal	IV
DD Breeding as cristate-prone; non-revertible	V

Fasciation

This is probably true of monstrose cerei, dealt with on p. 107. Recurrent mutations of an unstable gene could explain the erratic occurrence of fasciations in some plants.

Outside of succulent plants, the most familiar example of a cristate plant that has been selected to come true from seed is the cockscomb plant, *Celosia argentea* var. *cristata* (below). The spectacular display of its wavy pleated inflorescences in brilliant purple or yellow ensures it a place in horticulture. Perhaps the classic example of genes for fasciation being selected over a long period of time is the tomato. Wild tomato species in Mexico have small globular berries with a two-chambered ovary, as can be seen by bisecting one of today's cherry tomatoes. The first tomatoes to reach Europe in the sixteenth century had much larger ugly pleated fruits, the product of a type of fasciation. It took many years before these were accepted as delicacies or even as edible, but then selection began, retaining the genes for fasciation giving larger size, but moulding the berry into the smooth, near-spherical, multi-chambered fruit we now esteem. Some modern cultivars of strawberries have broad fasciated "fruits" valued for their size.

Returning to succulents, there is one striking example of a Type V cristate: the cactus described and named by Backeberg in 1934 and known today as *Echinopsis chamaecereus* 'Crassicaulis Cristata' (Figs. 82, 83). This probably arose as a mutation on the popular peanut cactus, has larger blooms and variously shaped crested stems, is self-compatible and comes true from seed (Hester 1940: 86). I have raised two generations of it from seed, and all seedlings became fasciated. It deserves further study; is it perhaps a polyploid?

Fig. 81 *Celosia argentea* var. *cristata* (right) from Lobel's Plantarum seu Stirpium Historia 126, 1576, and still grown today.

Opposite page:

Fig. 82 (Above) Two seed-raised plants of *Echinopsis chamaecereus* 'Crassicaulis Cristata'. Do not remove apparently normal growths: all are potentially capable of fasciation. (GR)

Fig. 83 (Below) *Echinopsis chamaecereus* 'Crassicaulis Cristata' in flower: normally at left, prodigally at right. (GR)

Fig. 84 (Right) Few succulents are more sportive in captivity than *Pachypodium lamerei*. Here the relatively thin, multi-pleated cristation is throwing frequent reversions to normal growth. (GR)

Fasciations in the Wild

One can buy from nurseries, beg from friends or go on safari and search, although times have changed since the days of carefree digging and slashing in habitat. That was how the first cristate and monstrose cacti came to the fore, and the fame of the sites of *Pachycereus (Lophocereus) schottii* in its monstrose guises in Baja California led teratophiles to make special field trips, eschewing the normal for the abnormal, the irreproducible, the exhibitable and the expensively resellable (Graham 1962). Certain areas in the S.W. U.S.A. became famous as rich in wild cristates (Lindsay 1962), and spawned the many theories on the cause reviewed previously on p. 8. As a result of five years "in quest of crests" Graham noted that where fasciations were common on one species of cactus, one could expect to find them on other cacti also. Near Barstow in Texas he found 75 plants of *Opuntia ramosissima* showing signs of fasciation, and Gates (1930) had reported similar experiences earlier. Such local concentrations of teratophytes add weight to the idea that at least the tendency to fasciation is inherited. Boke & Ross's classic study of 1978 on crest anatomy was made possible by finding an area in Oklahoma rich in differing crests on *Echinocereus reichenbachii*. A recent study of wild populations of cacti including teratophytes (but not the first, as claimed) concerns *Cereus hildmannianus* (alias *C. peruvianus* hort., *C. uruguayanus*) naturalised in Australia (Forster & Schneider 2000). Of 267 plants scored, 20.2% had cristate stems and 10.9% were monstrose.

Most succulentists on safari keep their eyes open for anything unusual, and I was certainly no exception. I was told that in a dense population of *Stenocactus (Echinofossulocactus) phyllacanthus* near Pachuca in Mexico crests were not uncommon, and sure enough one soon turned up (Fig. 85, p. 46). No doubt the biggest and showiest had found new homes long ago. Equally joyous was an encounter with a splendidly freaked-out *Larryleachia (Trichocaulon) cactiformis* hiding under shrubs in the Hester Malan Wild Flower Reserve at Springbok in South Africa (Fig. 86, p. 46). It was considerably larger in bulk than any of the normal plants of the same species in that area. An even more surprising find was a solitary *Pachypodium namaquanum* at Cauberg with its crown ex-

Fig. 85 *Stenocactus phyllacanthus* crest in habitat, not apparently disadvantaged by its lateral obesity. (GR)

panded into an oblique funnel-like crest topped with normal leaves and flowers (Figs. 87-89, p. 47). The serendipitous catalogue could go on. I was, after all, by now on the lookout, and if you look long enough and hard enough you may eventually be rewarded. Such was the case of *Bergerocactus emoryi*, which lines the roadsides for miles with its glorious columns of gold, as one drives through Baja California. My sudden squeal of rapture brought the car to an abrupt halt and my companions (Reid Moran and Len Newton) were led to see a single fan-topped stem (Fig. 90, p. 48). This one I did collect, unlike the foregoing, and it rooted back home and produced a new "fan" on top of the old (Fig. 91, p. 48). When later the "head" grew a nose and five fingers (Fig. 92, p. 48) I felt that it was showing its displeasure at being decapitated in no uncertain terms.

Fig. 86 *Larryleachia* (*Trichocaulon*) *cactiformis* cristate about 30 cm. wide and outstripping its fellows. (GR)

Fasciation

Fig. 87 (Above left) Len Newton examines a rare cresting *Pachypodium namaquanum* at Cauberg in 1971. (GR)

Fig. 88 (Above right), **Fig. 89** (Right) Close-up of the same crest showing normal flowers at the left and front. (GR)

Fig. 90 (Above) *Bergerocactus emoryi* lines the road for miles with its golden pillars in Baja California, but one stem decided to be different. Len Newton again scrutinises. (GR)

Fig. 91 (Below left) Back in captivity, the same crest grew a new "head and nose" on top of the original crest. (GR)

Fig. 92 (Below right)
Finally came four "fingers" and a "thumb"–surely it was trying to say something? (GR)

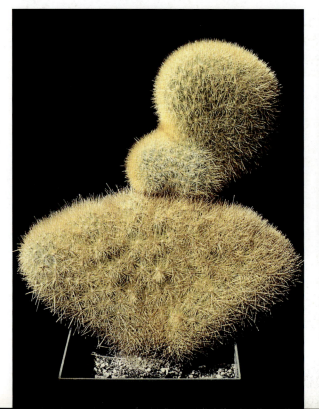

Fasciation

Figs. 93-95 (Top three) Some succulents are much more prone to fasciate than others. These crests of *Stenocereus* (*Machaerocereus*) *gummosus* were all photographed in one small area in the Baja California. (GR)

Fig. 96 (Bottom) Woody skeleton from a dead plant of the same. (LN)

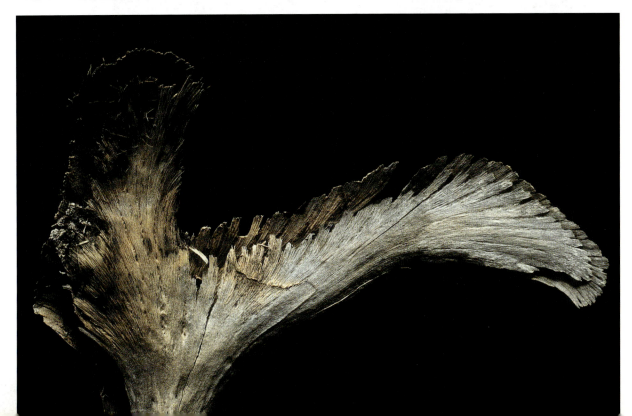

Interlude B

**CRISTATE CACTI IN HABITAT,
photographed in Mexico by R.N. Dehn
& G.F. Matuszewski and in South America
by Graham Charles**

Crested cacti are much sought by some collectors, and much photographed, so that one gets the impression that they are quite common in the wild. This is very rarely so, and for some species there is still no sighting of a cristate plant. But, like panning for gold, the searchers find them an irresistible challenge to locate. In the days when collecting was legal, old large crests like that of *Ariocarpus* on p. 52 did not take kindly to transplanting.

Cristate Cacti in Habitat

Fig. 97 (Above) *Mammillaria heyderi* ssp. *meiacantha*, San Luis Potosí. (RND)

Fig. 98 (Below) *Neolloydia conoidea*, Queretaro. (RND)

Cristate Cacti in Habitat

Opposite page:

Fig. 99 (Above) *Ariocarpus retusus*, Coahuila. (RND)

Fig. 100 (Below) *Mammillaria carnea*, Puebla. (RND)

Fig. 101 (Above) *Epithelantha micromeris*, Hipolito, Coahuila (?). (GFM)

Fig. 102 (Below) *Mammillaria grusonii*, Cerro Bola, Coahuila. (GFM)

53

Figs. 103, 104
(Above & below) *Lophophora williamsii*, La Peña, Coahuila. Old cristate plants may eventually grow larger than the equivalent normal plant, but they never compete and oust the normal species in the long run. (GFM)

Opposite page:

Fig. 105
Cereus jamacaru, Bahia, Brazil. (GC)

Cristate Cacti in Habitat

55

Fig. 106 (Above) *Pilosocereus gounellei*, Juremal, Bahia, Brazil. (GC)

Fig. 107 (Left) *Oreocereus celsianus*, East of Yavi, Argentina. (GC)

Opposite page:

Fig. 108 (Above) *Copiapoa cinerea* (*columna-alba*), Esmeralda, Chile. (GC)

Fig. 109 (Below) *Copiapoa rupestris*, San Ramon Valley, Chile. (GC)

Cristate Cacti in Habitat

Fig. 110 (Left)
Echinopsis (Lobivia) ferox, El Condor, Argentina. (GC)

Fig. 111 (Below)
Echinopsis haematantha (Lobivia chorrillosensis) Chorillos, Argentina. (GC)

Opposite page:

Fig. 112 (Above)
Eriosyce (Pyrrhocactus) bulbocalyx, Los Colorados, Argentina. (GC)

Fig. 113 (Below)
Eriosyce (Pyrrhocactus) umadeave, Santa Rosa de Tastil, Argentina. (GC)

Cristate Cacti in Habitat

Cactus&Co. *Teratopia*

Cristate Cacti in Habitat

Opposite page:

Fig. 114 (Above) *Gymnocalycium riojense*, South of Belen, Argentina. (GC)

Fig. 115 (Below) *Gymnocalycium saglione* var. *tilcarense*, Tilcara, Argentina. (GC)

Fig. 116 (Right) *Matucana aurantiaca*, West of Cajamarca, Peru. (GC)

Fig. 117 (Below) *Matucana formosa*, Balsas, Peru. (GC)

Fig. 118 (Left) *Matucana haynei* (*elongata*), Cordillera Negra. (GC)

Fig. 119 (Below) *Oroya borchersii*, Pumapampa, Perù. (GC)

Fig. 120 (Bottom) *Stenocereus gummosus*, near Santa Rita. (JP)

Variegation
chapter 2

Variegation as applied to plants is the local absence of green chlorophyll giving striping, banding, blotching or spotting of white, some shade of yellow, or other colour. Like albinism in animals, variegation in plants is possible, in theory at least, in any individual having chlorophyll, but there the similarity ends. A wholly albino plant is stillborn, lacking the chlorophyll essential to manufacture its own food. Such plants can be made to exist in cultivation, but only as grafts on green stocks (Fig. 121), and must be regrafted as soon as the stock starts to cork over. Most variegates we are concerned with here always have some green tissue, although it may appear quite small or masked beneath other pigmentation.

Variegates have a long history as garden curiosities, and nowhere more so than in the Far East, where the first books devoted exclusively to them were published in Japan in 1827 and 1829 (Hirose & Yokoi 1998) and specialist societies and journals exist for lovers of variegated ornamentals. They were the subject of much scrutiny in the early eighteenth century in Europe, and Bradley in 1718 gives a classic account of how leaf variegation could be transmitted from one plant to another by grafting. The Duchess of Beaufort was an enthusiastic collector of variegates in the late seventeenth century, and had 68 different kinds at Badminton, including the aeoniums illustrated in the figure below.

Fig. 121 *Echinopsis chamaecereus* (*Lobivia silvestrii*) 'Golden Peanut' with an apparently fully normal flower. Lacking chlorophyll, it relies upon a green stock for survival. (GR)

The eleventh Sort is a Variety of the tenth, which was accidentally obtain'd in the Gardens of the late Dutchefs of *Beaufort* at *Badmington*, from a Branch which broke off from one of the plain Sort of *Houfeleek* Trees by accident, and being planted in Lime Rubbifh afterwards, became beautifully variegated; from which Plant there hath been vaft Numbers rais'd, and diftributed into many curious Gardens, both at Home and Abroad. This is propagated in the fame manner as the former, and requires the fame Management in *Winter*; but the Soil in which it is planted fhould be one half frefh fandy Soil, and the other half Lime Rubbifh and Sea Sand, equally mix'd, in which it will thrive much better than in a rich Soil: You muft alfo be very careful not to give it too much Water in *Winter*, which will caufe it to caft its Leaves and decay. With this Management thefe Plants will grow to be eight or ten Feet high, and will produce beautiful Spikes of Flowers every Year, which are commonly in Beauty in *Winter*, and are thereby more valuable for coming at a Seafon when few other Plants do flower. Sometimes thefe Plants will produce ripe Seeds, which, if permitted to fall upon the Earth of the Pots, will come up the *Summer* following, from whence a great Stock of the Plants may be produc'd; tho' as they do fo eafily take Root from Cuttings, there will be no Occafion to propagate them any other Way.

Fig. 122 *Aeonium arboreum*, cultivated since classical times, with two variegated sports: 'Variegatum' [G. Don *Gen.Hist.* **3**: 123, 1834 has priority as cv. name] (left) which originated in the Duchess of Beaufort's collection in the seventeenth century and is figured here in her Badminton Florilegium. The other variegate (right) from the same collection seems to have no name and may be extinct. The contemporary text is from Miller's Dictionary 1731.

Colour in Plants

The colour that we see in plants owes its origin mainly to complex organic chemicals distributed in two different ways throughout some cells. In over-simplified terms, purple, red and blue shades arise from **cell-sap pigments** flooding the cell contents (Rowley 1997: 165). **Anthocyanins** are the most widespread, found in Crassulaceae and Asclepiadaceae, but in the Order Caryophyllales (Cactaceae, Aizoaceae, Portulacaceae, Didiereaceae) these are replaced by nitrogenous **betalains**. A change in pH of cell sap can alter the colouring, as happens when red petals turn blue as they age.

Green, yellow and orange shades are attributed to insoluble **plastid pigments** localised in **plastids**, more or less lens-shaped bodies scattered throughout certain cells. Green plastids are called **chloroplasts**, and contain **chlorophyll**, necessary along with light for the plant to synthesise organic compounds. In green leaf tissue there may be 30 to 500 chloroplasts per cell, and they have a certain mobility and can change orientation with the light. Yellow or orange plastids are **chromoplasts** containing **carotenoid pigments** - the basic colouring of carrots, lemons, buttercups and frailea flowers. Plastids arise from smaller, simpler bodies (proplastids) that are handed

Fig. 123 *Orostachys iwarenge* 'Fuji' with pale-margined leaves. (GR)

Fig. 124 *Echinopsis* showing the typical random patterning in most variegated stem succulents. (GR)

Fig. 125 *Senecio articulatus* 'Candlelight', a sport of the common "Candle Plant" with the deciduous leaves variegated. (GR)

on from generation to generation. It used to be thought that the nucleus with its chromosomes was solely responsible for perpetuating the species, but it is now known that the plastids contain a full complement of DNA and play a part. This is an important revelation, and explains some exceptions to the Mendelian laws of inheritance. Failure of the right plastids to pass through the egg cell into the embryo can lead to seedlings with little or no chlorophyll - a common happening in hybrid progeny.

Variegation

The best example in succulents of variegation involving more than one pigment is *Gymnocalycium mihanovichii*, the ubiquitous cactus of many colours (pages 66-69). The blackish-brown colour of the normal body results from looking at chloroplasts and chromoplasts through a wash of betacyanin. Eliminate the green chlorophyll, the carotin and/or the betacyanin and you would be left with the orange, pink or whitish patterning of the more extreme Japanese cultivars. It should be noted that a white appearance in some plants can result from minute air bubbles, as in snow, or from smaller chloroplasts, not to be confused with white wax on the surface.

Fig. 126 Early nineteenth century painting by Salm-Dyck of *Hylocereus undatus* 'Pictus', a golden stemmed mutant of the parent species. Once popular and available from nurseries, it seems to have been lost between the two World Wars. Like most variegates it was probably more delicate than the all-green type.

GYMNOCALYCIUM MIHANOVICHII: A FEAST OF COLOURS

Fig. 127 (Left) Frank Reinelt's selections of *Gymnocalycium*, bred for body colour, combining cell sap and plastid pigments. (GR)

Fig. 128 (Below) *Gymnocalycium* 'Hibotan Nishiki'. (HM)

Fig. 129 (Upper right) *Gymnocalycium mihanovichii* 'Pinkbotan', 'Kimbotan', 'Hibotan'. (GR)

Fig. 130 (Lower right) *Gymnocalycium* 'Hibotan Nishiki', showing chimerical stem sections. (GR)

Variegation

GYMNOCALYCIUM MIHANOVICHII: A FEAST OF COLOURS

Figs. 131-5 Pure colour variants in Harry Mak's collection. (HM)

Opposite page:

Fig. 136 (Above)
Gymnocalycium mihanovichii cristate. (SD)
and
Fig. 137 (Below)
a combination of fasciation and variegation in one grafted plant of the same. (HM)

Variegation

ANOTHER COLOUR EXTRAVAGANZA: ARIOCARPUS HYBRIDS
raised and photographed by Geoff Bailey

Variegation

Opposite page and below:
Figs. 138-141 *A. agavoides* x *A. kotschoubeyanus*. (GB)

Figs. 142-143 (Below) *A. agavoides* x *A. kotschoubeyanus*. (GB)

Opposite page:

Figs. 144-147 *A. retusus* x *A. scaphirostris*. (GB)

Variegation

Types of Variegation

Not all bi- and multi-colour patterning on plants is of equal concern here, and we must begin by distinguishing different types. As in fasciation, we can eliminate ephemeral or pathological types in favour of those more permanent and reproducible by horticulturalists.

I. Natural Variegation

Quite a few wild plants show a type of leaf variegation. *Aloe maculata* (*saponaria*) has pale spots on the leaves, and *A. variegata* has striking cross-banding or blotching. This is genetically controlled and quite normal; an all-green plant would be the freak. In cases that have been investigated, air bubbles over the green tissues are usually responsible. If these pallid areas serve any function, it is not obvious, but if they were deleterious they would certainly have been eliminated in the course of evolution. Sansevierias and bromeliads show many sorts of natural leaf variegation which adds greatly to their appeal. In passing, one should note another manifestation of variegation in flowers, where striped, spotted or multi-coloured petals are a positive advantage, rendering them more conspicuous and often providing guidelines to the nectar.

Fig. 148 *Aloe descoingsii* has naturally spotted leaves, as do many other aloe species. (GR)

Fig. 149 This strikingly yellow-striped 'Christmas Cactus' (*Schlumbergera* x *buckleyi*) was bought from a nursery as a variegated cultivar, but within two years of good cultivation all the chlorosis disappeared and it was wholly green again. (GR)

II. Chlorosis

This is a temporary pallor or blotching brought about by a lack of light or essential nutriments. Magnesium deficiency has been shown to be responsible for the yellow edges on the segments of the Christmas cactus shown in Fig. 149. The plants can recover if properly treated. Everyone will have seen the weak yellow growths on house plants (or succulents) kept in deep shade. Mineral deficiencies can often be detected by reference to the type of chlorosis produced, its colour, patterning and location. A healthy plant requires minute traces of iron, magnesium, copper, zinc, manganese, boron and other elements in just the right concentration.

III. Infectious Chlorosis

It has been known since the days of Richard Bradley (1718) that grafting a variegated jasmine on to a green jasmine stock could cause the stock to become variegated too. Today we recognise that a virus is responsible, just as it is in variegated tulips, where it is passed on not by grafting but by aphids that suck the sap. Among garden ornamentals, *Abutilon* mosaic is the most familiar example, but few other proven cases have come to light, and I know of none from succulents. For years I have been experimenting with *Pachypodium lamerei* 'Particolour' (Fig. 9), which looked like a virus with its random yellow patches and seasonal cycle of more or less green: even the main stem shows alternating bands of lighter or darker colour. But in spite of many grafts of stems or leaves on to four different all-green species of *Pachypodium*, none has ever shown the least sign of variegation, so I conclude that this is not caused by a virus but by an unstable gene (see below).

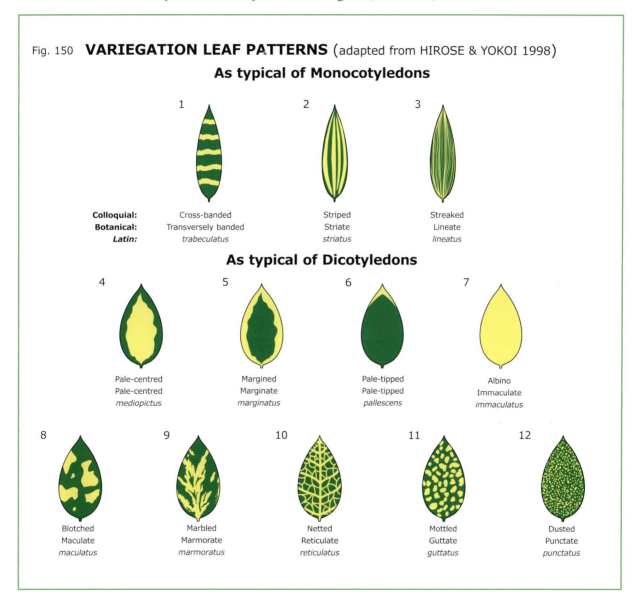

Fig. 150 **VARIEGATION LEAF PATTERNS** (adapted from HIROSE & YOKOI 1998)

IV. Genetically controlled (true) variegation

Here the pallid areas are more or less sharply defined and unaffected by nutrition, although the amount of sunlight may cause slight darkening or lightening. In leaves, the pattern reflects that of the veins, and, as we have already seen (p. 39), it differs for monocots and dicots. The former (Fig. 150, 1–3) have mostly long narrow blades with parallel veins, so become striped or streaked; rarely cross-banded. In dicots, with net-like venation, the effect is typically blotching or marbling (8–12) but can be marginal (4–5) or apical (6).

Sections through variegated tissue show that both green and clear cells contain plastids, but those in the latter type are smaller, swollen and lack chlorophyll. They never revert to normal, and their number can vary under different cultural conditions. The first comprehensive study of variegated succulents is that by Trelease (1908) on *Agave*, a genus in which many species have produced leaf striping, in some cases the most spectacular of all variegated succulents (Fig. 152). Trelease found that a normal green leaf has a 1.0–1.5 mm depth of green tissue on the upperside and rather less on the underside. The epidermis lacks chloroplasts except in the guard cells surrounding the stomata. The depth and extent of the chlorophyll-less tissue beneath determines the colour: white, cream or yellowish. Bright yellow is due to the presence of plastid pigments (flavones); pink to cell-sap pigments, anthocyanins. The pale areas are often sunken below the level of the green, perhaps on account of their parasitic nature and competition for food. Trelease quotes Roland-Gosselin in 1899 as claiming that for a variegated plant to be capable of leading an independent existence it must have at least one eighth of its usual complement of green cells. This explains why some very startling yellow offsets from agaves, haworthias and other succulents, have disappointed growers trying to multiply them.

Reciprocal Variegation

Variegation-prone leaf succulents often display the phenomenon of reciprocal patterning. Common examples in Crassulaceae are twin variegates of *Cotyledon tomentosa* (Fig. 151) and of *Crassula multicava* (Figs. 154, 155). In one there is a green leaf with yellow midstripe; in the other the colouring is reversed, with yellow edges and the centre green. One plant can arise from the other by a reversal of the green and non-green tissue layers in the meristem. It is also usual to find that plants with yellow edges throw an occasional all-yellow shoot; those with a yellow centre are more prone to revert to all green.

Fig. 151 *Cotyledon tomentosa*, reciprocal variegates: 'White Palm' ('Cream Topping') (left) and 'Yellow Palm' (right). (GR)

Variegation

Fig. 152 Agaves provide some of the most striking examples of leaf variegation, none more diverse, stable and long cherished than those of *A. americana*. From left to right: 'Marginata', 'Mediopicta', 'Striata' and 'Mediopicta Alba'. (See p.82) (GR)

Fig. 153 *Crassula multicava* 'Variegata' produces easily detachable bulbils on the inflorescence that reproduce the variegation. (GR)

Fig. 154 (Above) *Crassula multicava* 'Panache'. (GR)

Fig. 155 (Left) *Crassula multicava*: the reciprocal variegate 'Variegata'. (GR)

Opposite page:

Figs. 156-157 Variegation in dwarf *Euphorbia suzannae* takes the form of blocks or large flakes of yellow, suggesting the action of an unstable gene. A cristate cultivar of this, 'Maelstrom', is in cultivation. (GR)

Unstable Genes

Another type of genetically controlled variegation results from the vacillations of an unstable gene, that, for reasons known only to other genes, switches chlorophyll production on or off at will. The outcome is whole blocks or smaller patches of white or yellow tissue distributed at random among the green. A good example in succulents is in *Euphorbia suzannae* (Figs. 156, 157), which also exists as a cristate 'Maelstrom' (Fig. 444). *Pachypodium lamerei* 'Particolour' (Fig. 9) seems to be of the same origin too.

Unstable nuclear or chromosomal genes are not uncommon in garden ornamentals, and most commonly associated with parti-coloured flowers (*Mirabilis jalapa* provides striking examples). *Echinopsis* 'Johnson's Gold' (Figs. 158, 159) is a yellow-flowered variant of the peanut cactus that often shows a stripe or segment of reversion to orange on its flowers.

Variegation

Figs. 158, 159 *Echinopsis* 'Johnson's Gold' showing flecks, stripes and whole segments of orange. (GR)

Origin

Seedlings devoid of chlorophyll are often encountered, especially from hybrid seed, but they normally perish as soon as the food reserves in the seed are exhausted. All-yellow cacti can be preserved, however, if tip-grafted on *Pereskiopsis*, and then thrive as long as the "nurse root" remains green. The fact that such grafts have a limited life unless re-grafted every few years has led to many being unloaded from oriental sources upon unsuspecting customers giving cacti a bad name as difficult to keep. One special case, the "red gymno", has already been figured (pp.66-69).

In addition to arising from seed, variegations can appear as sports (somatic mutations) anywhere about the plant: the tip of a leaf, one side of a stem, or a whole shoot. In the third case one has a chance of preserving it by removing the shoot and treating it as a cutting.

Trelease raised 425 bulbils from the inflorescence of *Agave fourcroydes*-the normal, unstriped species. Of these, 18 showed some degree of variegation. However, with subsequent growth only one proved sufficiently well-marked and constant to be of garden value.

The origin of variegation is as much shrouded in mystery as that of cristates. We are never present at the moment of conception. The attractive pink-and-cream *Senecio kleinia* 'Candystick' (Fig. 160) arose in my glasshouse in London in the early nineteen-fifties. A large normal plant in the bed had died back to ground level and was given up for lost. However, the following summer new shoots began to sprout from the callus covering the stump. One of these had a pallid streak on one side. I removed all the normal shoots and, by judicious pruning, eventually eliminated all side branches except one coming out from the pale area. This produced the handsome cultivar that has been propagated (very slowly) and distributed, and only very rarely reverts to type. But the same variegation I have since seen in another collection, where it had an independent origin.

Induced and inherited variegation

Unlike cristates, variegates have been produced artificially. The market for yet more highly coloured foliage plants, and their enormous popularity in the Far East, led to attempts to sabotage the production line for chlorophyll and genetically modify the plant. Radiation and chemical mutagens are the chief tools, aided by micropropagation. Hirose & Yokoi (1998) illustrate a new *Hosta* cultivar generated by X-rays, but I have yet to hear of any succulents successfully transmuted in this way. Undoubtedly the means exist if the demand warrants the effort.

Another source of novelty is from seed. Way back in 1731 Philip Miller, in a lengthy essay on variegation, noted strains of sweet pea and maple that bred true from seed for variegated foliage. Clearly this is genetically controlled. Other examples are *Rohdea*, a popular house plant, that exists in a range of variegated cultivars raised from seed in Japan, and a true-breeding variegated *Dracaena* is also known.

Mostly, however, seedlings from variegated plants revert to all-green colouring. Why this is so will be evident from the next chapter on chimeras. In 1954 I raised numerous seedlings from seed of *Yucca aloifolia* 'Variegata' from the Jardin Exotique in Monaco. Not one showed the least stripe of yellow.

In the belief that variegation in *Haworthia* is inherited through the cytoplasm of the female parent, Hirose (2000) gives details of a back-crossing programme using a variegated haworthia as female parent, and reports some measure of success.

Fig. 160 *Senecio kleinia* 'Candystick', selected out as a stable periclinal chimera from a single pale-striped sprout from a dying stump. (GR)

Anatomy: a case of split personality

No succulent is more suitable to introduce the study of variegation than the ubiquitous *Agave americana*, which has obliged with a range of variegates during more than three centuries of cultivation (see Figs. 152 & 161). The commonest and best known, with golden yellow edges to each leaf is 'Marginata' (Trelease 1908), and it arose as a sport in Beaumont's garden in the Hague. Many other variegations of *Agave americana* have arisen, some even more showy than this, and several have been given latinised names, some of which are upheld by Gentry (1982, p.281). However, they merit no more than cultivar status, especially as some (notably 'Striata') are unstable and occasionally interchange. To put the record straight I append a key to the commonest, along with the cultivar name (Jacobsen 1974) and a rather wild guess at the date of origin or first mention in the literature.

Agave americana Variegates

A Striping marginal only		
B Margins white to creamy, sometimes flushed rose	'Marginata Alba'	1690
BB Margins yellow	'Marginata' ('Marginata Aurea', 'Picta', 'Variegata')	Pre-1714
BBB Margins pale green	'Marginata Pallida'	19th century
AA Striping central; margins green		
C One central creamy-white stripe	'Mediopicta Alba'	19th century
CC One central yellow stripe	'Mediopicta' ('Mediopicta Aurea')	1834
CCC More than one cream to yellow stripes	'Striata'	1834

The different leaf patterns reflect the location of the different cell lineages and the ways they sort out from the leaf primordium. In essence we are dealing with a composite organism composed of two genetically different tissues packaged as one – a **chimera**, in fact. And chimeras are so exciting that they deserve a whole chapter to themselves, so they shall have one.

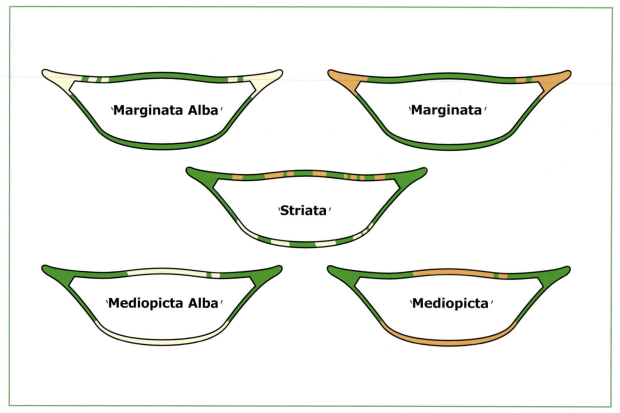

Fig. 161 Sections of leaves of striped cultivars of *A. americana*, showing the locations of green and non-green tissues, after Trelease (1908). See p. 77.

Variegation

Fig. 162 Teratophytes mingle with the crowd in a large nursery. (SR)

Fig. 163 Commercial production of red gymnos. (SR)

Interlude C
The Colour Freak-out

Variegation results not from the creation of new colours but the local suppression of existing colours, notably of green chlorophyll. It adds novelty to a collection, and can turn a normally rather plain green specimen into a real eye-catcher and artistic tonic. Note in the following selection how the patterning differs between leaf and stem succulents, reflecting the different cell lineages arising from the meristem.

The Colour Freak-out

Fig. 164 (Above) A choice *Agave potatorum* 'Bonanza' in Doris Sharp's collection in Reading. (GR)

Three variegated haworthias in Harry Mak's collection in Manchester:

Fig. 165 (Right) *H. cuspidata*. (HM)

Fig. 166 (Below left) *H. viscosa* hybrid. (HM)

Fig. 167 (Below right) *H. attenuata* variety. (HM)

The Colour Freak-out

Opposite page:

Fig. 168 (Above) *Gasteria gracilis* variegated. (HM)

Fig. 169 (Below) *Aeonium* 'Harry Mak', a striking variegation worthy of wide distribution. (GR)

Fig. 170 (Above right) *Aeonium* 'Sunburst'. (GR)

Fig. 171 (Right) *Sedum sieboldii* 'Mediovariegatum'. (GR)

Fig. 172 (Below) *Euphorbia tirucalli* 'Sticks on fire', ISI 93-38. (HM)

Fig. 173 (Below right) *Schlumbergera* x *buckleyi*, a true stable variegation (cf. Fig. 149). (HM)

The Colour Freak-out

Opposite page:

Fig. 174 (Above) *Lophophora williamsii* variegated. (HM)

Fig. 175 (Below) *Astrophytum asterias* x *myriostigma* variegated. Note the blotchy or mottled effect in dicot stem succulents. (GR)

Fig. 176 (Above right) *Astrophytum asterias* variegated. (HM)

Fig. 177 (Right) A variegated *Mammillaria*. (HM)

Fig. 178 (Below right) *Mammillaria marksiana* with reduced or locally absent chlorophyll. (SR)

Fig. 179 (Above) *Echinopsis (Lobivia) densispina*, a red variegate. (SR)

Fig. 180 (Left)
Orocereus celsianus variegated, 15-20 years old and 25 cm tall. (MC)

Fig. 181 (Below) *Parodia (Notocactus) mammulosa* ssp. *submammulosa* variegated. (HM)

Chimeras
chapter 3

Fig. 182 Chimera in Greek mythology had the head of a lion on a goat's body and the fiery breath and rear end of a dragon.

"First, dire Chimera's conquest was enjoin'd; A mingled monster of no mortal kind!
Behind, a dragon's fiery tail was spread; A goat's rough body bore a lion's head;
Her pitchy nostrils flaky flames expire; Her gaping throat emits infernal fire."
–HOMER: The Iliad VI.

In botany, a plant **chimera** contains a mixture of two or more cell lineages, each of which retains its genetical identity while dividing to form tissues without any blending of hereditary material (Tilney-Bassett 1986). The name is taken from Homer's awesome monster, which it will be noted was female, despite the lion's mane, although we shall never know more of the nature and breeding behaviour of this unique species. For the next line reads: "This pest he slaughtered ...." – a tragic early setback for the conservationists.

Origin

To understand how variegation arises, we must go back to Fig. 40 and follow the course of dividing cells at the tip as they go on to form different strata of tissue. In short, three layers of cells are produced: a **skin** (tunica), a **middle layer** and a **core** (corpus) filling the whole of the centre. A simple analogy is a hand wearing two gloves, one over the other (Fig. 183). The top two layers are initially one cell thick, the upper constituting the **epidermis**. Later they may thicken by divisions parallel to the surface, as in the margins of leaves, where the "icing" overflows the cake. Each layer once initiated preserves its genetic individuality unchanged and without blending with others. The epidermis is always colourless except for the guard cells of stomata (breathing pores), but by looking at leaf edges where its underlying cells may contain chloroplasts one can tell whether the skin layer is classifiable as green or non-green.

Mutations probably occur frequently at the meristem, but are almost invariably unfavourable and quickly smothered by healthy cells. A mutation suppressing manufacture of chlorophyll can survive, first as a chain or cluster of cells, later as a line, streak or broader sheet. Close inspection of any plant usually reveals occasional yellow or white streaks, but they are of as little consequence to the plant's welfare as a dimple on the cheek.

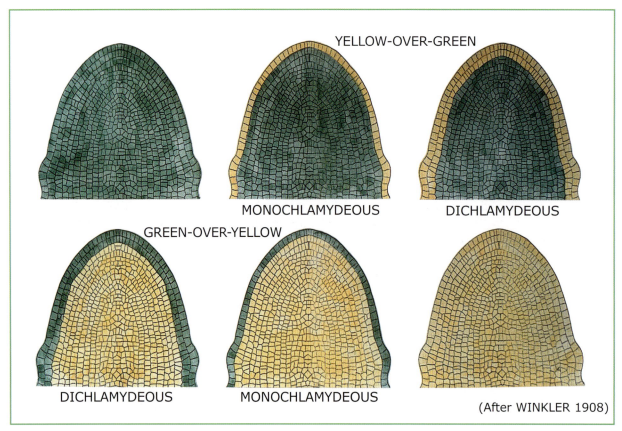

Fig. 183 Types of periclinal chimera. Mono- and di-chlamydeous distinguish one- and two-celled surface layers. The eye perceives the colour blend from one layer over another.

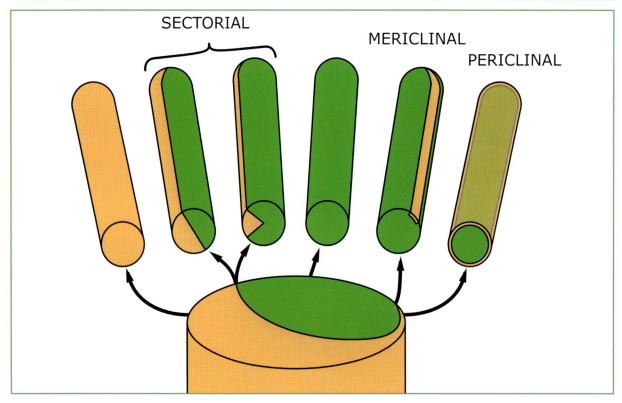

Fig. 184 Cross-section of a hypothetical chimerical stem showing branches arising from differing compositions. Sectorial and mericlinal chimeras are unstable like the original; periclinal chimeras are the most durable.

Chimeras

Figure 184 shows the cross-section of a plant stem near the apex in which a considerable part of the stem has developed without chlorophyll. It is our classical chimera: an organism combining a mix of two related but dissimilar tissues, one the fully functional green prototype, the other the rogue lacking chlorophyll. In appearance the stem would have a horizontal stripe of green and another of yellow. It would be unstable and has no future as such. Left to itself the green tissue would outgrow the parasitic yellow portion which would be lost.

What is of interest here is the branches that grow from this stem. Branches have a deep-seated (endogenous) origin (see fig. 296) and so carry up with them all three meristematic layers of tissue. According to where these branches arise, so different combinations are possible. Figure 184 shows six of these and the terms used to describe them. All-green and all-yellow shoots are self-explanatory; the latter is inviable unless grafted on a green stock. **Sectorial** and **mericlinal chimeras**, like the parent stem, are unstable, although they may be preserved by selective pruning, and some, such as *Agave americana* 'Striata' are established in cultivation. Some striking new variegates can arise from their vacillations.

Of maximum concern here is the rare generation of a **periclinal chimera**, in which a bud has grown out at exactly the right point to carry up a complete layer of one type of tissue over the other (the skin alone, or skin plus middle layer). Periclinal chimeras are stable. Some never revert, others do so occasionally when a bud emerges from the core alone, or from the skin, as following damage to the surface. Most variegated cultivars in cultivation are periclinal chimeras (Tilney-Bassett 1986).

Fig. 185 Combinations of green (G) and white (W) in a three-layered chimera with named examples within tall *Sansevieria trifasciata* and dwarf *S. trifasciata* Hahnii Group. (After Chahinian 1993 & Tilney - Bassett 1986).

Fig. 186 Five variegated mutants of the ubiquitous *Sansevieria trifasciata* (right): 'Laurentii' (left), 'Hahnii', 'Silver Queen' (centre), 'Golden Hahnii' (upper) and 'Silver Hahnii' (lower). (GR)

Returning to the original concept of a meristem generating three concentric layers of tissue, we find that a mutation suppressing chlorophyll can affect any or all of these three layers. Where this occurs, up to eight different patterns of variegation are possible according to how the strata combine. No succulent shows this better than *Sansevieria trifasciata*, a familiar (over-familiar?) house plant that even in the wild has attractive natural pale cross-banding and mottling (Fig. 186). In captivity it has an extraordinary tendency to sport not only variegates but differences of habit (dwarf, leaf widths, etc.) (Chahinian 1986).

Figure 185 displays the eight possible mixtures of genotype and how they might have arisen from a mixed meristem. In describing them, **G** refers to a green layer and **W** to white or yellow. Chahinian (1992–1994) has done outstanding research in identifying the clones in cultivation corresponding to different combinations of layers, although the cultivar names in common usage do not all fully accord with the ICNCP. Ignoring the inviable albino, all seven types have been recognised and named in *S. trifasciata*, and seven more in its dwarf mutant group 'Hahnii'. The full story is more complex, including mericlinal and sectorial chimeras, as well as variegates of just about all the other species of the genus (Chahinian 1993).

Identifying the stratification of a given variegate is made difficult by the upper layers masking the colour of the core. Chahinian (1999) gives guidance on holding the leaves up against a strong light to perceive the contrasted colours within. Leaf cross-sections should be consulted also, and leaf margins which derive from the skin layer alone.

Chimeras, being mechanical mixtures of two genetically distinct tissues, cannot breed as such. In this they are quite different from hybrids, and the old term "graft hybrids" was misleading and should be dropped. It turns out that in the formation of gametes (sex cells) the uppermost skin layer plays no part. It is the middle layer that participates, although some exceptions have been recorded (Tilney-Bassett 1986: 59). Inherited variegation is of a different nature, although I know of no examples in succulent plants.

Chimeras other than variegates

Variegation is but one expression of chimerical make-up in plants, one that is immediately recognisable. Many other sorts of chimera are to be found; indeed, they are probably quite common, but show no visible symptoms so pass undetected. For instance, there are "**mixoploids**", plants having cells of more than one chromosome number. This is true of *Sansevieria trifasciata* 'Laurentii', where the yellow skin layer, in addition to lacking chlorophyll, is tetraploid, with larger cells standing above the surrounding green tissue.

It could be that some of the most puzzling naturally occurring plants that baffle taxonomists are **cryptic chimeras**: genuinely different, but unique and irreproducible. If nothing else, this gives a warning, if warning were needed, not to name a "new species" from a single specimen!

Chimeras can arise from a mutation at a stem apex, but unlike crests and variegates they can also be manufactured. And the possibilities are limited only by what two plants can be grafted together. How this is done is shown in Fig. 187. A large number of grafts are made (1) and, when united, cut across horizontally to expose the maximum area where the two tissues abut (2). All normal shoots that grow out subsequently are nipped out in order to encourage one to arise exactly on the line of the graft (3), carrying up tissues of both components (4, 5). This can then be propagated and selectively pruned to try to obtain the stable periclinal form of chimera.

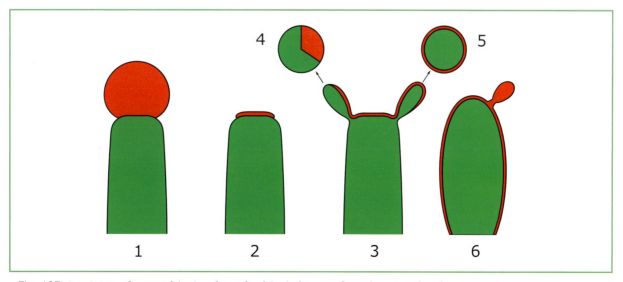

Fig. 187 1-6. Origin of sectorial (3,4) and periclinal (3,5) chimeras from the point of graft union, and reversion of periclinal chimera to one component (6).

Chimeras

Examples of a disorganised mixing of tissues of stock and scion following grafting

Opposite page:

Fig. 188 (Above) *Echinopsis + Ariocarpus scaphirostris* chimera. (FXS)

Fig. 189 (Below) *Ariocarpus kotschoubeyanus* transmuting. (FXS)

Fig. 190 (Right) Another grafted specimen derived from *Ariocarpus kotschoubeyanus*. (FXS)

Few plants are easier to graft and more suitable to chimera production than stem-succulent cacti and pachypodiums, yet it is another bizarre fact of history that they have been totally overlooked. All the pioneer work on making and interpreting chimeras has been done with tomatoes, potatoes and garden shrubs. In the bigger commercial nurseries of Europe, America and the Far East we have the ideal set-up where cactus-grafting is practised on a large scale. When a scion dies off but leaves a thin skin covering the stock there is the maximum likelihood of a shoot emerging combining both stock and scion. It was not until I made inquiries that I found that this does, in reality, happen. Mr Hirao in Japan tells me that he has seen a number of sectorial chimeras of *Ariocarpus kotschoubeyanus*, *Epithelantha micromeris*, *Gymnocalycium denudatum* and *G. mihanovichii* following grafting on *Echinopsis*, some of which he went on to describe and illustrate in *Shaboten* **25**: 8–9, 1960. More recently some of these have been figured by Kobahashi (2000). All showed mixtures of the features of both stock and scion, but monstrosity reaches its ultimate horror-movie peak in what has been christened +*Hylogymnocalycium* 'Singular': the + signifies chimera, as distinct from x for sexual hybrid, and the "generic" name is a compound of the two parental generic names, *Hylocereus* and *Gymnocalycium*. Can you imagine a more unlikely partnership? Certainly there is no chimera on record, past or present, to match it (see Figs. 191-197, Rowley 1989, 1997b, 2005). Whatever one's feeling about the preservation of such curios, the scientific interest is considerable in observing how two so different tissues interact when forced to exist side by side. First, a word about the parents.

The stock is the tender *Hylocereus* (*H. undatus*, probably) beloved of prosperous oriental nurseries because it usually dies off the first winter unless kept extra warm, leaving the customer to crave for a replacement. On its own it is a vigorous climber, with triangular, green jointed shoots bearing aerial roots, which in nature attach to rocks or tree trunks and carry it high in the air. The scion is the familiar "red gymno" whose official title is *Gymnocalycium mihanovichii* B. & R. var. *friedrichii* Werd. f. *rubra* hort., otherwise 'Hibotan' or 'Ruby Ball'. The parent species has a curious dark banded plant body owing its hue to a mixture of three pigments: red betacyanin, yellow flavones and green chlorophyll. Eliminate the chlorophyll and you have the orange-red colour of 'Hibotan'. But there are many other colour variants of the same species in shades of pink, yellow, almost white, dark green and particoloured, no doubt resulting from different colour deletions and blends from the original palette: see pp. 66-68.

Now look at the pictures of +*Hylogymnocalycium*. Ignore all the small 'Hibotans' which are reversions arising from the skin component. The body of the chimera consists of short joints with three or sometimes more rounded angles and areoles bearing spines intermediate between those of the two components. The green surface has blotches of deep purple - the red of 'Hibotan' over the green of *Hylocereus* (Figs. 194-197). How do we know that the layers are not the other way round? Simple: there are occasional aerial roots breaking out from between the ribs (see Fig. 191). Roots arise endogenously, that is, from deep within the stem and in any case I have never seen a *Gymnocalycium* bearing aerial roots. Reversions to the core component are rarer, but unmistakably recall *Hylocereus*. Assuredly +*H*. 'Singular' will be much studied in the future as it provides ideal material for identifying the two components of a chimera.

+*HYLOGYMNOCALYCIUM* 'SINGULAR'
('Rainbow dragon')

Chimeras

Opposite page:

Fig. 191. (Top) +*Hylogymnocalycium* 'Singular' resulting from a *Gymnocalycium* 'Hibotan' that swallowed its grafting stock, *Hylocereus*. Now both components compete to determine the look of the plant. Note the aerial root, coming from the *Hylocereus* within. (GR)

Fig. 192. (Middle left) +*Hylogymnocalycium* shows frequent reversions to 'Hibotan', the skin component, which should be removed if the chimera is to be preserved. (GR)

Fig. 193 (Middle right) +*Hylogymnocalycium* with typical 'Hibotan' flowers from reverted offsets. No other flowers have been reported. (GR)

Fig. 194 (Bottom) Cross-sections of stems of +*Hylogymnocalycium* showing different amounts of green *Hylocereus* at the core. (GR)

Figs. 195-197 (Upper - Middle - Lower right) +*Hylogymnocalycium* 'Singular' - the two components visibly battle for supremacy. (HM)

The birth of a new chimera has been well documented by Bill and Yvonne Tree, two celebrities of the cactus world to whom I am indebted for information and pictures. They write in perfect unison: "A *Uebelmannia pectinifera* seedling was grafted on *Echinopsis* stock. The graft was successful and the scion grew to about 2 cm. After a number of years I noticed the stock had rotted and the rot had also gone into the scion. I managed to save a small piece which I successfully grafted on to a *Cereus* stock. As it began to grow I realised it was strange and had the colour and some of the features of the *Uebelmannia* but the form of an *Echinopsis*." Subsequent behaviour is totally in line with that of a chimera having a layer of *Uebelmannia* tissue over a core of *Echinopsis*. The flowers (which would arise from meristematic cells below the surface) are like those of *Echinopsis*. This chimera is stable and reproducible from offsets, so deserves a name: + *Uebelechinopsis* for the partnership of *Uebelmannia* and *Echinopsis*, and 'Treetopper' as a cultivar name for a tophole introduction by the Trees.

Fig. 198-200 + *Uebelechinopsis* 'Treetopper' (BYT)

Chimeras

Chimeras

A few probable, if not 100% certain, chimeras in succulents have been described, aside from the numerous examples of variegation. In Crassulaceae we have *Sempervivum* 'Grigg's Surprise' (Byles 1957), with bizarrely twisted leaves that reverts to *S. tectorum* var. *calcareum*, and *Sempervivum* 'Oddity' which looks as if it could be another chimera; *Sedum rubrotinctum* 'Aurora' (Pusey 1962), a colour variant of *S. rubrotinctum* and *Echeveria* 'Hoveyi' (Keppel 1971) which occasionally throws shoots of *E.* 'Zahnii', a "straight" cultivar of hybrid origin. *Harrisia* 'Jusbertii', a cactus of garden origin unknown in the wild, on rare occasions sports shoots or segments of stems with much larger spines that look indistinguishable from *H. bonplandii*, a respectable indigen (Drawert 1983). *Echinopsis* 'Haku-Jo' (Fig. 205) is another example (Rowley 1980). This attractive Japanese cultivar has curious bands of fine white felt linking the areoles along the rib crests, but small abortive flowers. Every now and again part reversions in stem or flowers suggest that it is a chimera derived from one of the common *Echinopsis* hybrids or species (*E. multiplex*, maybe) with a mutated epidermis. Drude De Looze sent me the photograph (Fig. 206) of a sectorial *Astrophytum* hybrid, with and without white scales: a treasure indeed for the collector of such marvels as there is no way it can be propagated!

Opposite page:

Fig. 201 (Above) *Sempervivum* 'Grigg's Surprise'. (HM)

Fig. 202 (Below) *Sempervivum* 'Oddity'. (HM)

Fig. 203 (Right) *Echeveria* 'Hoveyi'. (HM)

Fig. 204 (Below) *Echeveria* 'Topsy Turvy'. (HM)

Fig. 205 (Left) *Echinopsis* 'Haku Jo' showing the upper sector reverted to normal without the furry crest. This could be a chimera or the product of an unstable gene. Flowering is rare, but in typical fashion for a chimera can be of two types: short abortive blooms lacking a proper perianth, and long more typical echinopsis blooms presumably emerging from core tissue (see pictures in *Piante Grasse* 22: 168, 2002). (GR)

Fig. 206 (Below) A sectorial *Astrophytum* hybrid with scaly and scaleless sectors. (DDL)

Monstrosities
chapter 4

Too easily we take for granted that every seed will grow up into a normal plant exactly like its forebears. Because it goes on in silence, unseen and at a molecular level, the unfolding programme is rarely given a passing thought. Yet if we knew its full complexity, in terms of chemistry and coding, sequences and metamorphoses, I suspect that it would make sending a rocket to the moon look relatively simple. Like any long and complicated recipe, a glitch at any stage can set the whole operation off course, usually with fatal consequences. Here it is the rare non-fatal glitch that we are after; the one pearl that could be grown from one itchy oyster.

Whole books have been written categorising and describing all the assorted freaks and wonders of plant teratology (Masters 1869; Wordsell 1915–1916). Here a few examples are selected and illustrated to given an idea of the range available in succulents. Most of the changes, like fasciation, involve a reduction in symmetry, and negative features such as the reduction or loss of parts (leaves, spines, ribs) (Fig. 207). We start with lesser departures from normality, wherein the plant is still recognisable at least as to genus.

ASSORTED CACTUS MONSTERS:

Fig. 207
(Back row, left to right)

Mammillaria bocasana 'Caterpincy'

x *Sclerinocereus* 'John White' (*Echinocereus knippelianus* x *Sclerocactus* (*Toumeya*) *papyracanthus* – a wide cross

Mammillaria spinosissima 'Swordfish'

(Front row, left to right)

Mammillaria 'Fred'

Astrophytum myriostigma 'Onzuka'

Copiapoa humilis var. *hypogaea* looks monstrose but isn't

Cleistocactus strausii 'Quantum Leap'

Mammillaria 'Freaky'
(GR)

NON-MONSTERS:

Fig. 208
Euphorbia tortirama (Rear); *Sarcocaulon peniculinum*, *Cintia napina* & *Eriospermum dregei* (Front).
(GR)

What are called **monstrosities** in botany are well shown by *Cereus* 'Abnormis', brilliantly painted by Salm-Dyck around 1805 (Fig. p. 260) as *"Cactus abnormis"* and described as such by Willdenow in 1813, although its origin is unrecorded, and there are several synonyms. It is most commonly encountered as *"Cereus peruvianus monstrosus"*. The five or six normally straight ribs are disrupted and branching is irregular and more frequent. This is often referred to as an example of fasciation, and indeed some of the sideshoots may show crested tips, relating the two phenomena. True cristation must be rare in *Cereus*; one example is shown on p. 55. Gigantic specimens of 'Abnormis' can be walked under in the Jardin Exotique at Monaco or the Huntington Botanic Gardens in California (Fig. 211). Growth is vigorous as in the type, and normal-looking flowers and fruits are freely produced. The plants vary in appearance, and the reason became clear when I received seed of 12 differently named cerei from the Huntington Botanic Garden and scored the seedlings (Rowley 1954; Figs. 212, 213). Only 3 accessions bred true in the sense of producing no teratophytes. Eight produced 5% to 67% monstrose seedlings. The twelfth was *"C. peruvianus monstrosus"*, and behaved differently from the others. Germination was low, and a higher percentage died in infancy. But of 21 sur-

Fig. 209 (Upper left)
Cereus variabilis 'Monstrosus'. (HM)

Fig. 210 (Left)
Cereus 'Abnormis'. (HM)

Opposite page:

Fig. 211 (Above)
Monstrose *Cereus* in the Huntington Botanic Garden, California, where many flower and fruit freely. (GR)

Fig. 212 (Below left)
Genetic variation in *Cereus* seedlings.

Fig. 213 (Below right)
C. hildmannianus 'Monstrosus', 5 seedlings.

Monstrosities

vivors, 9 were shrubby - monstrose and 2 dwarf - monstrose. The dwarfs looked far removed from a normal cereus, and grew exceedingly slowly. After 50 years one is about 70 cm tall and the other 25 cm. Of course, all this seed was open - pollinated and probably highly hybridised, but it does at least show that in *Cereus* this kind of monstrosity is genetically controlled, and requires no obvious stimulation to cause it to manifest.

Most celebrated of all cactus teratophytes, both for their beauty and for uniquely existing in the wild, are those derived from *Pachycereus (Lophocereus) schottii*. The weird totem - pole stems lack spines and ribs and produce no functional flowers; only the rare reversions confirm that they are indeed *P. schottii*. Three populations exist in Baja California: the first near El Aroc with over a thousand plants of the thick - stemmed variant 'Monstrosus' (Fig. 214), another at Rancho Union,

'Mieckleyanus' with thinner stems that tend to show ribbing and look nearer the type (Lindsay 1963). A new location for 'Mieckleyanus' was found 350 Km to the south in 2002 (Cact.Suc.Mex. 47:87-90, 2002). These sculptures in jade are keenly sought after by collectors, and being very slow to grow or branch, they have been ruthlessly over-collected. Yet they survive to make us wonder how such extraordinary, sterile monsters obtained a foothold in the first place. They make up in vigour for what they lack in armature, and in favourable conditions, as at the Desert Botanical Gardens in Phoenix, Arizona, form magnificent shrubs (Fig. 50). Some think that in the wild they gradually spread from the rooting of fallen branches, but the totem-pole cactus remains every bit as much a mystery as it looks.

Fig. 214 (Left) Most statuesque of all teratological cacti, *Pachycereus* (*Lophocereus*) *schottii* 'Monstrosus'. (GR)

Fig. 215 (Below) *Pachycereus* (*Lophocereus*) *schottii*: top of a barren stem (left), flowering stem (right) and 'Monstrosus' (centre). (GR)

Figs. 216, 217 (Bottom left & right) *Mammillaria bocasana* 'Fred' leading its disorganised existence. (HM)

Monstrosities

A few other columnar cacti occasionally throw bizarre sports similar to the *Lophocereus*. That of *Echinopsis lageniformis* (*Trichocereus bridgesii*) (Fig. 218) rarely fails to evoke comment. The cavalcade of grotesquerie ends with miniatures like 'Fred', reputedly derived from the polymorphic *Mammillaria bocasana* (Figs. 216, 217), although a similar amoeboid oddity in Jerry Barad's collection in New Jersey (Fig. 221) seems to be reverting to *Echinocereus*. Looking at these strange almost conophytum-like blobs of green, one recalls the masses of callus produced in tissue culture and the efforts of operators to trigger them off into differentiating plant bodies. Here we seem to see the process in reverse: retrograde de-differentiation. Some startling red spineless cristates of *Echinopsis* are illustrated in Kakt.u.a.Sukk. 56: 95-96, 2005.

Fig. 218 (Below left) *Echinopsis* 'Jock, Dick & Willy' is as vigorous as the normal species, *E. lageniformis* (*Trichocereus bridgesii*), but, like Bottom, "Bless thee! Thou art translated." (GR)

Fig. 219 (Below right) Fasciation and monstrosity often combine, as in this *Euphorbia fruticosa* erupting into randomly branched crested heads. (GR)

Fig. 220 (Bottom left) Variants of *Crassula muscosa* (*lycopodioides*): 'Cristata' in the centre; to left and right two different clones of 'Monstrosa', and at the front shoots of the wild parent species (GR171) for comparison. (GR)

Fig. 221 (Bottom right) *Echinocereus* 'Fred' identifiable only by the reversion at the left. (GR)

Figs. 222, 223 *Myrtillocactus* monstrose in Tony Mace's collection. (DM)

Morbid or moreish?

The frontier between what we find attractive and what repels us as malignant is sometimes quite arbitrary. The "diseased" striped tulips and variegated abutilons have already been mentioned. Cactus growers sooner or later may come across a tumour-like outgrowth on one of their pet plants (Figs. 224, 225), often covered in downy wool or colourful abortive flower buds. I have detached and grafted some of these, and the survivors eventually grew out and reverted to normal growth suggesting that the host cells were outgrowing a pathogen. A dramatic picture gallery of tumours that nobody could love is given by Dubrovsky (2002), who found many of the native cacti in the south of Baja California (*Pachycereus pringlei* especially) to be scarred with amorphous corky tumours 3 - 80 cm in diameter, some accompanied by a hemiparasitic mistletoe, *Phoradendron diguetianum*. He compares them to crown galls produced by *Agrobacterium tumefaciens* in non-succulents.

Fig. 224 Abnormal sideshoot on *Mammillaria karwinskiana*, perhaps pathological. (GR)

Fig. 225 Galls like this on *Ferocactus horridus* are pathological. If grafted, eventually normal growth will resume. (GR)

Proliferation

A normal plant is covered in meristems, one at the tip of each branch and in the axil of every leaf. Formation of shoots and other organs has been shown to be controlled by the ratio and interaction of plant growth regulators: cytokinins and auxins. Normally all but a few meristems are held in check, but if that control is released, every one grows out or attempts to do so as far as its food supply permits. The result can be a strange cauliflower-like exuberance of growth (Figs. 227, 229) that we call **proliferation**. The term is further used for any unnatural extension of growth, as a shoot growing out of a flower, or one *Opuntia* fruit growing on top of one another.

Proliferation has nothing to do with fasciation, and it is regrettable that the two terms are often confounded. One thing certain about the types of proliferation commonly found in cacti is that it is pathological. Studies on *Opuntia tuna* 'Monstrosa' led to the isolation of a mycoplasma (an infective body combining features of bacteria and viruses but lacking a firm cell wall) responsible for the condition (Jeffries & Smale 1971). Gräser in 1960 had shown that when this plant is grafted upon a normal *Opuntia orbiculata* ("*O. senilis*") as stock, that also began to proliferate from its areoles. Other types of proliferation give rise to the witches' brooms seen on trees and shrubs, where *Corynebacterium fascians* is responsible, and similar symptoms can be induced by treatment with cytokinins. Mark Dimmitt has photographed perhaps the ultimate in decorative proliferation in *Ferocactus wislizeni* (Figs. 232, 233) where every areole sprouts symmetrically round the stem. He has also kindly provided pictures of a similar aberration in *Stenocereus* (Figs. 234, 235) and even, tentatively, in *Carnegiea* (Fig. 236).

Fig. 226 (Top) *Opuntia ovata (russellii)* proliferous. (HM)

Fig. 227 (Centre) *Opuntia microdasys* proliferating. (GW)

Fig. 228 (Bottom) *Opuntia* 'Maverick', another example of proliferation. (GR)

Opposite page:

Fig. 229 (Top left) *Disocactus* x *mallisonii* (x *Aporoheliocereus smithii*) proliferating: every bud on every shoot attempts to grow. (GR)

Fig. 230 (Top right) A curious type of proliferation in *Leuchtenbergia principis* in which offsets appear at the tips of tubercles. (GR)

Fig. 231 (Bottom) *Escobaria minima* proliferous. (HM)

Monstrosities

Figs. 232, 233 *Ferocactus wisilizeni*, with the "Brussels sprout mutation" - proliferous areoles all over. (MD)

Figs. 234, 235 (Below & below right) The same aberration in *Stenocereus thurberi* and 236 (Bottom right) to a lesser extent in *Carnegiea gigantea*. (MD)

Spiral torsion

Rare treasures indeed can arise when a normally straight-ribbed cactus becomes spirally twisted, presumably by differential growth of the axis and cortex, the latter growing faster. The effects can be exciting and novel, but few collectors, alas, possess them (Rowley 1985/6). The genus *Cereus* is again source of the most frequently seen examples (Figs. 237, 238). Other tall columnar cacti occasionally oblige with tight helices or gentler curves. Some stem succulents have naturally spiralled ribs - one thinks of *Euphorbia tortirama* and *E. groenewaldii* (Figs. 239, 240). Here a straight - ribbed specimen would be the freak. Rauh & Lavranos described a var. *tortirama* of *Euphorbia cactus* with all its branches twisted in a helix. It formed an extensive stand of many plants in the Wadi Maadin northwest of Aden. However, Len Newton found two normal plants of *E. cactus*, each with a single mutant spiralled branch. This type of spiralling presumably has no adverse effect on survival. *Aztekium* presumably achieves its venerable wrinkles by foreshortening of the axis preventing expansion of the swelling ribs.

In large nurseries where cactus seedlings are raised by the million, it pays to scrutinise the seed-pans at an early stage and put aside anything that does not conform, grafting if necessary to help its survival. In this way some really astonishing deviants can come to light (Figs. 242, 243). I photographed these in Dutch nurseries. The *Copiapoa* was one of a cherished pair, twisting in opposite directions but I was able to see only this one. The other disappeared a week earlier following a visit from a coach party from a country I'd rather not mention! At least it shows a high value put upon such miniature gems. The ultimate in spiralling cerei grows in the Berlin Botanic Garden and is illustrated in *Piante Grasse* 25 (1): 10, 2005.

Monstrosities

Opposite page:

Fig. 237 (Left) Spiral torsion in *Cereus* 'Vortex': note that spiralling can take place in either direction. (GR)

Fig. 238 (Right) A more extreme example of spiralling in *Cereus* 'Vortex'. Unfortunately such wonders are hardly ever offered by nurseries. (GR)

Figs. 239, 240 (Above & above right) As consolation, some succulents are naturally spirally twisted, as in *Euphorbia groenewaldii*. (GR)

Fig. 241 (Right) *Acanthocereus tetragonus*: a curious mutant, part monstrose, part spiralling. (GR)

Masters (1869) cites 49 different cases of spiral torsion, none in succulents but mostly from the European flora. Two remarkable examples come from the genus *Crassula*, where leaf and shoot arrangement throughout the genus follows an inflexible opposite and decussate plan: "crossed pairs" all the way up the axis. Spiral rosettes are achieved in a few species by a gradual twisting of successive leaf pairs. But in two species a radical departure from this regularity occurs - sometimes. One form of *C. capitella* habitually throws inflorescences that look as if it has had an accident in a blender (Fig. 246), resulting in a badly wrung neck. Often these are accompanied by normal inflorescences on the same plant. The phenomenon has long been known, and a specimen showing spiral torsion was exhibited at a meeting of the Royal Horticultural Society in London by Mrs. Vera Higgins in 1949.

For over 30 years I have nursed a clone of *C. orbicularis* that can carry torsion further to produce wondrously scrolled inflorescences in the flat (Fig. 244) or as a hollow tube (Fig. 245). In both species the flowers look quite normal and the freak displays appear as healthy as the norm. I have found that the performance is related to nutrition: potbound or starved plants, if they flower at all, produce only normal inflorescences. If you want a gala performance, repot them in rich soil, and pamper them with water and warmth.

Fig. 242 (Above) *Copiapoa cinerea*, one of a pair of extravagantly spiralled seedlings turning in opposite directions. (GR)

Fig. 243 (Left) Another unique example of what might be called the "blender syndrome": *Parodia* (*Notocactus*) *crassigibbus*. (GR)

Opposite page:

Fig. 244 (Above) *Crassula orbicularis* var. *rosularis* with a normal, opposite, decussate inflorescence (left) and a freak spiralled one (right). (GR)

Fig. 245 (Below left) Spiral torsion in *Crassula orbicularis*. (GR)

Fig. 246 (Below right) Spiral torsion in *Crassula capitella*. (GR)

Monstrosities

Spinelessness

Spine suppression or reduction is rarely encountered – presumably as a recessive mutation – in cacti (Figs. 247, 249) and a few such deviants are in commerce. However, spinelessness occurs as the norm in certain wild taxa, notably *Echinocereus*:

	Armed	**Unarmed**
E. coccineus (*triglochidiatus*)	f. *coccineus*	f. *inermis*
E. scheeri	ssp. *scheeri*	ssp. *gentryi*
E. viereckii	ssp. *viereckii*	ssp. *morricalii*

These pose an evolutionary problem: if spines have any protective value in the wild, how do these spineless plants escape being eaten? The answer probably lies in chemical protection: alkaloids have been isolated from some species of this genus (Rowley 1997a: 247).

Fig. 247 (Left) Spine suppression, more or less complete, occurs in some variants of *Echinocereus* (GR)

Fig. 248 (Below) The ubiquitous "golden barrel" (*Echinocactus grusonii*) has sported variants in spine colour, cristation and spinelessness, but never more bizarre than this combining spine reduction, fasciation and monstrosity. (GR)

Monstrosities

Fig. 249 (Above) *Rebutia krainziana* 'Prodigy', offered in the trade as "var. *breviseta nuda*". The flowers never expand properly. (GR)

Fig. 250 (Right) *Opuntia ficus-indica* 'Eyeful' combines variegated pads with proliferous areoles – and lives to tell the tale. (GR)

Fig. 251 (Below right) *Echeveria gibbiflora* 'Carunculata'. The tumour-like outgrowths on the leaves are a turn-on for some, a turn-off for others. (GR)

Foliar follies

A few curious outgrowths of leaves have found favour and been preserved as cultivars. They presumably owe their origin to mutations. Most familiar is *Echeveria gibbiflora* 'Carunculata', which produces extraordinary brain-like excrescences at the base of most of its leaves (Fig. 251). Seeds from self-pollination were raised at the John Innes Horticultural Institution in 1924 and about a quarter of these came up with warted leaves (Fig. 252). Crisped leaf margins are found in some Crassulaceae, notably various species of *Echeveria* (Fig. 253).

A pair of leaves may sometimes fuse to form a pitcher (ascidium) at the end of a shoot (Rowley 1947), or single leaves may become pitcher-like, as if the margins were jointed together. That strange and provocative phenomenon *Crassula* 'Gollum' (Fig. 254) is a sport of the common 'Jade Plant' (*C. ovata*) in which no two leaves seem to be exactly alike, and it comes true from leaf cuttings.

That very variable giant *Kalanchoe beharensis* has produced one cultivar 'Fangs' with toothlike protuberances on the leaf undersides. But in some succulents horny outgrowths from the leaf surface are quite normal, notably *Faucaria tuberculosa*.

Fig. 252 (Above) Seedlings raised at the John Innes Horticultural Institute in 1924 from *Echeveria gibbiflora* 'Carunculata'. 6 of the 19 show carunculations.

Fig. 253 (Above right) *Echeveria crenulata*, a cultivar selected for exaggerated crisping of leaf margins. (GR)

Fig. 254 (Below) *Crassula ovata* (*portulacea*) 'Gollum', oddest aberration of a widely grown and variable species, unique in leaf form a good bonsai or house plant. (GR)

Double flowers

Double flowers have some or all of the stamens, and often the styles as well, replaced by petal-like organs. When no trace of reproductive organs remain we call the flower full. It is of course also sterile and incapable of further breeding. So abundant in all types of garden ornamentals, double flowers are hardly seen in succulents, largely because nobody has looked for them. The best example is in *Portulaca grandiflora*, the popular bedding annual that has for long been bred for larger and more colourful blooms (Fig. 255). Some of the epicacti and *Echinopsis* hybrids approach doubleness with an increase in number of inner tepals, and a few stapeliads have been photographed with extra petals or even a complete second corolla (White & Sloane 1937 3: 1123). Of curiosity value only is *Gasteria* 'Double Carver' (Brandham 1974), a hybrid with ugly misshapen blooms with 7 to 11 tepals. A semi-double sport of *Mammillaria guelzowiana* is illustrated in *Cact.Succ.J.N.S.W.* 20: 148, 1997.

Fig. 255 Flowering doubling is rare in succulents - because nobody has looked for it. *Portulaca grandiflora* is one exception. (GR)

Micropetaly

What might be called micropetaly is the phenomenon of suppressed petal expansion, seen in Cactaceae in a few cases where the normal perianth is replaced by a ring of tiny linear scales. *Echinopsis* 'Stern von Lorsch' (*Kakt.u.a.Sukk.* 33: 195, 1982 & 54: 237, 2003) is an example, probably derived from *E.(Lobivia) densispina* or *rebutioides*. An earlier case deceived Backeberg into describing it as a new genus and species: *Delaetia woutersiana* (an invalid name), but it is actually a variant of *Eriosyce taltalensis* with suppressed perianth.

Hybrids

Hybridisation alone does not qualify a plant for inclusion in this "rogue's gallery". However, few teratophiles could resist the sheer oddness of, say, the wide cross *Echinocereus knippelianus* x *Sclerocactus* (*Toumeya*) *papyracanthus* (Fig. 256) with its assortment of different spines, disorganised growth and abortive flowers, or the celebrated x *Ferobergia* (*Ferocactus* x *Leuchtenbergia*), in which some ('Gil Tegelberg', Fig. 257) add variegation to their novel looks.

Combining two genotypes in one cell inevitably tends to give imbalance, and it is no surprise to find that many teratophytes are of hybrid origin, although the evidence for this is mostly circumstantial. Certainly, the amateur addicted to cross-pollinating every flower that opens in his glasshouse has a good chance of unleashing monsters upon the world, if that is what he wants.

Miscellanea

The catalogue of deviants among cultivated succulents could go on almost indefinitely as popular demand leads to efforts to detect and increase variability. In Japan, where interest has never been higher, whole books have been published recording in pictures and text the range of diversity within a single genus (*Ariocarpus*, *Astrophytum*, etc.) or even a single species (*Haworthia truncata*). Mention has already been made of the book on cultivars of a single species of *Sansevieria*, *S. trifasciata* (Chahinian 1986). For the addicted teratophile, there is source material around if you can hunt it out. Locating it is the problem. Contact through the succulent societies and study groups is an ideal start, leading to specialist nurseries and private growers. Journals, newsletters and round robins are a help, and with electronic means of communication becoming ever more dominant, national frontiers are no barrier to locating the most remote sources.

Opposite page:

Fig. 256 (Above) x *Sclerinocereus* 'John White' from Bradley Batch Cacti shows a bewildering diversity of spines from needlelike to flat and hooked, random branching and abortive flowers. (GR)

Fig. 257 (Below) x *Ferobergia* 'Gil Tegelberg' acquired variegation as well as a form intermediate between the parent genera, *Ferocactus* and *Leuchtenbergia*. (MS)

Fig. 258 (Above) Bizarre happenings on a grafted crest of *Echinocereus pulchellus*. (GR)

Fig. 259 (Right) In large populations of wild species one comes across occasional freak growths, as in these constricted stems of *Pachycereus fulviceps*. (GR)

Interlude D
Monstrosities

Under this heading it is convenient to include all those aberrations that cannot be obviously assigned to any of the other categories. No doubt they have many and varied genetic origins: "misprints" in the great floral library, and collectible in the same way that a stamp collector seeks out and treasures rare malfuctions of the printing press. But, unlike stamps, they are living things, by-products in the march of evolution, and serve to remind us, if nothing else, of the immense wastage of non-survivors that preceded any successful species alive today.

Fig. 260 *Cereus* 'Abnormis', painted by Salm-Dyck around 1805 as *"Cactus abnormis"*.

Fig. 261 and Fig. 262 Two further *Astrophytum* oddities - nature's outcasts. (HM and GR)

Fig. 263 (Above) A spectacular group of monstrose *Astrophytum myriostigma* in a Californian nursery. (SR)

Fig. 264 (Below) *Cleistocactus strausii* 'Quantum Leap': one of several monstrose variants of the popular white-spined columnar species, and unique in its wave-like patterning. (GR)

Figs. 265, 266
+ *Hylogymnocalycium* 'Singular' (Above) and *Mammillaria* 'Fred' (Middle).
No two specimens are alike, so no apology is needed for over-indulgence. (GR)

Fig. 267 (Below) *Pachycereus* (*Lophocereus*) *schottii* 'Mieckleyanus'. (HM)

Opposite page:

Fig. 268 (Above) *Opuntia mamillata* crest, since the 1930's affectionately known as the boxing glove cactus. (HM)

Fig. 269 (Middle) *Mammillaria prolifera* 'Rocky Hill'. (HM)

Fig. 270 (Below) *Parodia ottonis* monstrose. (HM)

Monstrosities

Fig. 271 (Above left) *Rebutia marsoneri* (*krainziana*) 'Haywire'. (GR)

Fig. 272 (Above right) *Sclerocactus mesae-verdae*, barely recognisable in disguise. (SD)

Fig. 273 (Below) A monstrose *Sedum* from the New York Botanical Garden. (HM)

Two for the Price of One
chapter 5

The seemingly infinite capacity of gene programming does not limit plants to a single brand of teratology. Sometimes two of the aforementioned growth aberrations are combined within one individual, with results even more wondrous to behold. It seems appropriate to end with a list of some of these compound freaks, as a stimulus to readers to come up with more of their own. Now who is going to be the first in the field with a "three-in-one"?

	FEATURES	AUTHORITY
	C = Cristate	HY = Hirose & Yokoi 1988
	M = Monstrose	R = Rowley herein
	P = Proliferous	S = Sato 1998-1999
	V = Variegated	SS = Suguri & Sato 1996
CACTACEAE		
Ariocarpus fissuratus	CV	SS
Ariocarpus kotschoubeyanus	CV	S
Astrophytum asterias	CV	S
Aztekium ritteri	CV	S
Cereus hildmannianus (*peruvianus*) 'Yellow Lion'	MV	HY
Discocactus horstii	CV	S
Echinocactus 'Moelleri'	CV	S
Echinocactus texensis	CV	S
Echinopsis eyriesii 'Two-step Art'	CV	HY
Echinopsis multiplex	CV	S
Echinopsis tubiflora	CV	S
Epithelantha micromeris	CV	S
Ferocactus glaucescens	CV	S
Frailea castanea	CV	S
Geohintonia mexicana	CV	S
Gymnocalycium anisitzii	CV	S
Gymnocalycium fleischerianum	CV	S
Gymnocalycium gibbosum	CV	S
Gymnocalycium hossei	CV	S
Gymnocalycium mihanovichii	CV	HY
Gymnocalycium mostii	CV	S
Gymnocalycium ochoterenae	CV	S
Gymnocalycium ochoterenae	MV	S
Gymnocalycium pflanzii	CV	S
Gymnocalycium quehlianum	CV	S
Gymnocalycium saglione 'New World Crown Brocade'	CV	HY
Gymnocalycium schickendantzii	CV	S
Gymnocalycium spegazzinii	CV	S
Mammillaria magnimamma	PV	S
Obregonia denegrii	CV	S
Opuntia ficus-indica 'Eyeful'	PV	R
Parodia mammulosa	CV	S

	FEATURES	AUTHORITY
EUPHORBIACEAE		
Euphorbia ingens	CV	S
Euphorbia lactea 'Spring Horse'	CV	HY
Euphorbia neriifolia 'Giraffe Horn' (Reputedly in Japan since 182'7)	CV	HY
Euphorbia suzannae 'Maelstrom'	CV	R
CRASSULACEAE		
Aeonium arboreum 'Crested Sunburst'	CV	HY
Crassula ovata 'Gollum'	MV	S
ASTERACEAE (COMPOSITAE)		
Senecio kleinia 'Candystick' cristate	CV	R

The above list makes no pretence to be complete. There are other examples with only Japanese cultivar names, or nameless, or ephemeral one-offs. A recent publication by Harry Mak, his "Photo Album of Succulents in Color Vol. 3" (2003), describes and figures 81 new cultivars, many of them teratophytic.

Two for the Price of One

Opposite page:

Fig. 274
Echinopsis chamaecereus 'Rainbow Fan', a variegate of 'Crassicaulis Cristata'. (HM)

Fig. 275 (Upper Right) *Gymnocalycium* 'Hibotan' cristate. (HM)

Fig. 276 (Below) *Mammillaria gracilis* 'Bunty', a popular and vigorous clone in cristate guise. (HM)

Two for the Price of One

Opposite page:

Fig. 277 (Above) *Opuntia ficus-indica* 'Eyeful'. (HM)

Fig. 278 (Below) *Euphorbia neriifolia* 'Giraffe Horn' variegate and cristate. (HM)

Fig. 279 (Top right) *Euphorbia suzannae* 'Maelstrom' variegate and cristate. (HM)

Fig. 280 (Right) *Aeonium* 'Sunburst' variegate and cristate. (HM)

Fig. 281 (Below) *Echeveria* 'Topsy Turvy' crest. (HM)

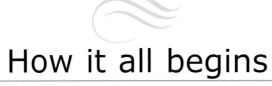

How it all begins
chapter 6

"Why has my cactus gone funny?" is a question commonly asked when a sudden change in growth pattern is spotted, followed by "Is it something I have done?" "Is it diseased?" "Infectious?" and sometimes "Is it rare?" or "How much is it worth?". Some questions are more easily answered than others. But the big issue: why and how plants suddenly change their life-style, won't go away. To answer with feigned authority "It's genetical, you know" or "A mutant" may suffice to quell curiosity, especially if backed up with a string of acronyms: GM, DNA, CAM and so forth. But the truth is that any answer takes us back step by step to the origin of life itself, and there we have an instruction manual lacking the first page. Even if we knew all the answers it would be as difficult to present them in simple language as it would be to explain how a video camera works to someone brought up in an isolated jungle.

Yet there is enormous satisfaction in trying to unravel the secrets of nature as every step, however small, adds a piece to the great jigsaw puzzle and stimulates the search for more. Thus, in seeking the origin of cristates, for example, we find some tantalising clues from very different fields of research. Fasciation and spiralling involve an upset to the normal balance of cell division. Workers in Japan have identified a mutation of one or two proteins that control the shaping of the microtubules of the cell wall causing twisted or lop-sided growth: the beginnings of a slant, or spiral, or fasciation perhaps. And what initiates changes in anatomy such as this? Some recent research from Machado *et alii* (2000) may give a hint. They raised plants from tissue culture of an apparently normal *Cereus* and interpreted its mutations to monstrose growth as isoesterase variants suggesting crossing-over between chromosomes in somatic cells - an interchange of genetic material normally confined to meiosis (that is, directly preceding pollen and egg cell formation).

This is called **somaclonal variation** and has been observed in various plants raised in tissue culture that differ from the parent plant. Different chemical agents can stimulate this type of change, taking us a step nearer, but not arriving at, the origin of mutations. As yet this is the only such research I know of dealing with succulents, but it is highly significant. We could be nearer an explanation for many observations of anomalous growth hitherto only expected in sexually reproduced seedlings.

Since Wolthuys propounded the enigma in his popular handbook of over half a century ago, it has become clear that although environmental factors (mechanical injury, shock, nutrition) can trigger off teratological growth, there must be the right genetical background there in the first place. Most, perhaps all, higher plants possess the latent ability to fasciate or variegate, although some have yet to express it. The tendency is widespread, and not confined to flowering plants: fasciation can occur in some conifers (*Sequoia*, *Cryptomeria*, *Araucaria*) and ferns (leaf dissection). To learn more of the factors bringing about these changes, we can turn to the parallel and better documented research on the changes in a meristem leading to the initiation of flowering. First the plant has to reach a certain age and degree of maturity. Then flowering can be triggered by a combination of external stimuli, notably temperature and day length (photoperiod), and the interaction of at least four genes encoding proteins that determine the identity of sepals, petals, stamens and carpels. Fasciation and variegation may have a similarly complicated background scenario.

It is hard to visualise the complicated formulae operating within a meristem to determine stem dimensions, rib number, tubercle size and shape and a multitude of other features. Easier to conceive is how a gene malfunction anywhere along the line can dramatically alter the final shape and symmetry. Most such mutations are retrogressive, arresting or distorting development of major organs. Monstrose succulents reveal the outcome of such rare aberrations, from simple spine suppression to the most disruptive changes, as in the celebrated *Mammillaria* 'Fred' (Figs. 216, 217, 221) where the whole plant body develops little beyond an undifferentiated callus. Results to the eye can be abhorrent or alluring, as when a new dimension in architectural or sculptural beauty is revealed.

It is interesting in this context to note the long-running controversy over the use of genetical engineering to create new organisms. If the more extreme teratophytes considered here had been first offered to the public as man-made triumphs of genetical manipulation rather than wholly natural phenomena, what would the reaction have been?

Naming
chapter 7

All teratophytes are treated as cultivars, even if first collected in the wild (indigens). They do not form wild populations or breed true in the sense that species do, or are supposed to. The majority in cultivation are single clones. Thus any names given to them fall under the ICNCP (International Code of Nomenclature for Cultivated Plants, 2004). However, all are referable to species or genera, and the names of these are covered by the ICBN (International Code of Botanical Nomenclature, Greuter *et alii*, 2000), as well as those of intergeneric hybrids and chimeras.

Since Linnaeus, teratophytes have been informally indicated by adding a suitable Latin adjective after the binomial, such as *cristatus*, *variegatus* or *monstr(u)osus*. The meaning was self-explanatory, a condensed description, just as *flore pleno* translated as "with a full (i.e. double) flower". This system worked well with botanists and gardeners until outlawed by the ICNCP which banned Latinised names for cultivars after 1958 and insisted that "fancy" names in modern languages be given instead. Pre-1959 valid Latinised names can be retained as cultivars, as for example *Opuntia cylindrica* 'Cristata', described at least as early as 1865 by Carrière (who incidentally called it "pope's feet"). But searching out the earliest publication of each name takes much time and toil as there is no collective index or guide. This also leaves a great many later cultivars without an acceptable name under the codes (Rowley 1997c).

Hence not all the names in this book will stand the test of time if the Codes are to be observed. In general, Latinised names known to have been in use long before 1959 have been taken up at the cultivar level, and new names given only when the subject is a new or widely circulated without any acceptable name. Finding good descriptive names that accord with the Codes is far from easy. 'Crested' and 'Variegated' are out as they are adjectives, not nouns. 'Crest', 'Cristate', 'Variegate' and 'Monster' can be used as nouns, with or without embellishments. In general the Americans have been the most adventurous and inventive at finding apt names for cultivars, as witness Harry Johnson's nursery catalogues and Juan Chahinian's striped sansevierias. By way of a footnote one might add that the Codes themselves are subject to change every five years or so, and since each change leads to increased complexity and occasional backtracking, their aim of nomenclatural stability is not yet in sight.

Fig. 282 Cristates in the Grootscholten Nursery in the Netherlands. (GR)

It is worth mentioning that some past species names are not what they seem. *"Adromischus cristatus"* is not fasciated, *"Copiapoa marginata"* and *"Pachycereus marginatus"* are not striped, and *"proliferus"* in names such as *"Mammillaria prolifera"* means merely freely offsetting. Engelmann's *Echinocereus engelmannii* var. *variegatus* is not variegated; the spines are differently coloured.

Anyone can christen their own novelties provided that they study the ICNCP first, abide by the rules and publish the necessary documentation to establish the identities of the new cultivars. No Latin is necessary, although pictures and a voucher specimen (preserved) are advisable. However, before plunging in one should stop to ask if a new name is really necessary. There is no point whatever in giving a name to a one-off freak that can never be propagated or distributed, and is equally unlikely to crop up again. Distribution is the important factor, and the first priority is to work up a supply of the novelty for sending to nurseries or specialist growers. In the process, which may take years, you may decide that it is not so novel after all, or has received a name already. But at least by waiting you will not have burdened the literature with yet another unwanted name, and there are far too many of those already.

Fig. 283 *Cereus* 'Vortex' – an amazing case of spiralling. (JC)

Cultivation
chapter 8

A few specialists grow nothing but cristates or variegates or both, and spend their lives building up fantastic collections of oddities that look as if they came from another planet (Figs. 3, 284, 285). However, for most succulent fanciers the teratophytes are in the minority, adding lustre and a touch of bravura to an otherwise orthodox collection – if succulents can ever be described as orthodox. Few collections are without one or two, although the owner might be unaware of their nature, or try to hide them, blushingly admitting when challenged that he doesn't really approve of pathological freaks.

We can assume that all teratophiles began with a love of normal succulents, and are therefore con-

Fig. 284 Andreae's collection of cristate cacti in Germany. (GR)

Fig. 285 Cristate cacti, mostly grafted, in a British glasshouse. (GR)

versant with their growth requirements as distinct from tomatoes or trilliums. Here only a short resumé will be given, with emphasis on differences from the routine management of succulents in the home and glasshouse. For those starting from scratch, there is a wide selection of primers available from bookshops, including the following:

A. £5 or under

INNES	Cacti & Succulents	1988
IVIMEY-COOK	An introduction to Cactus & other Succulent Plants	1984
MOTTRAM	Growing Succulent Plants in Captivity	1998
NOLTEE	Cultivation table for Succulents	1999
NORTHCOTT	An Introduction to Cacti & other Succulents	1995
PILBEAM	How to care for your Succulents	1984

B. £8 or under

CHAPMAN & MARTIN	Exotic Cacti	1989
KEEN	Cacti & Succulents	1990

Back in 1731 Philip Miller noted that variegated plants tend to remain smaller than all-green, are more cold-sensitive and shorter lived. In bright sunlight yellowing tends to intensify; white is more likely to burn and cork over. Sun-scorch is a bigger risk for variegates than ordinary plants, whereas too much shade dims the contrast in colour. The experienced grower learns how to get the balance right, with a few casualties along the way. Because they have less chlorophyll than usual, with the pallid areas parasitic upon the green, variegates would be expected to need more cosseting in captivity. The same is true of cristates and monsters in general, which have lost their balanced architecture, perfected for the job it has to perform, and must compete at a disadvantage if they are to survive at all.

However, there are notable exceptions. *Agave americana* 'Marginata' is as prolific, durable and resistant as the type, and only slightly less hardy. The same can be said of the garishly yellow-blotched

Fig. 286 (Left) Propagation of *Echeveria* 'Easter Bonnet' from leaf cuttings. Both these plants came from the same leaf; that on the right is a new cultivar with darker leaves. (GR)

Fig. 287 (Above) Sectorial split in *Agave americana*. Offsets would be worth saving as potential new stable variegates. (GR)

Opposite page:

Fig. 288 Another attractive wide cross: x *Alworthia* 'Fantasy' (*Aloe bellatula* x *Haworthia* sp.), with marginal striping. (GR)

Cultivation

variegate of *Euphorbia abyssinica* (*E. erythraeae*). The monstrose variants in *Cereus* mostly grow, flower and fruit like normal plants despite looking so different. In the duller, humid climate of northern Europe the branch-cristate variant of *Euphorbia woodii* (*E. flanaganii*) outgrows both the head-cristate and the normal plant, as if it had re-invented *Epiphyllum* cladodes on quitting the deserts. The outcome is that nobody should be put off starting a collection of teratophytes by fears that they are a pampered lot and that too much time and money will be wasted looking after them. To press the point home, I append a list of types recommended for beginners (pp. 278-279), followed by another of more challenging sorts to act as a spur to the would-be connoisseur.

Siting

Whereas cristates in general are happiest in a frost-free glass-house similar to that for their non-cristate next-of-kin, variegates provide us with some of the best of all house plants: colourful even in absence of flowers, tolerant of partial shade, dry air and erratic watering. They should thrive so long as they are not frosted, and some will even brave it out over a radiator where little else would endure for long. *Sansevieria* tops the list, although the variegates of only one species, *S. trifasciata*, are at all common. *Peperomia magnoliifolia* 'Green & Gold' has claims to be a succulent, as do *Cordyline* and *Dracaena*, abounding in variegates, and *Yucca*, many of which are full hardy and contribute much to garden design.

In cold climates the high cost of keeping a glasshouse or conservatory frost-free in winter impels most growers to get away with the least amount of heat needed to save the contents from extinction. And a surprising number, apart from Madagascan and tropical African species, survive a winter minimum of around 5°C (40°F). Economy measures include lagging the glass with bubble plastic in winter, arranging the plants so that seedlings, propagations and delicate types are nearest the heat source, and bringing the most tender treasures indoors for the winter on to sunny windowsills. It is a general belief that dry, dormant succulents tolerate cold better than those turgid and in full growth.

For those not constrained by the cost of rising fuel bills, a little extra heat can work wonders for some

Fig. 289 *Aeoinium arboreum* 'Zwartkop' ('Black Cap'), a superb dark colour variant. (GR)

plants. I recall the incomparable Heidelberg University Botanic Gardens in the sixties, where the tropical houses had the heating full on even at the height of summer. On the other hand, high mountain cacti are used to winter cold, snow even sometimes, and may fail to bloom if denied their dry, cool resting period.

Soil and non-soil

The growing of pot plants under glass has changed little as regards potting medium since the John Innes Horticultural Institution standardised sterile, loam-based composts and in the U.K. Fison's countered with loam-free (sand + peat) mixes to which chemical nutrients were added. Choice today depends partly on the availability of good, well matured loam. Coir and other peat substitutes have been favoured by some as less damaging to the environment. At all events, teratophytes like any other succulents demand a porous, readily draining medium, especially if on their own roots rather than grafted. How porosity is achieved is immaterial: by added grit, broken brick, pumice, perlite, vermiculite or specially prepared mineral products. If water lingers in the top of the pot after watering, it is time to unpot and change the compost. Silt blocking the drainage outlets is a common problem: put the coarsest particles at the bottom of the pot, or cover with coir or similar inert material to act as a filter.

Crests that sprawl over the surface of the soil are best elevated on grit or small pebbles to avoid lying on wet soil too long. Grafted teratophytes can stand a richer mix (John Innes No.3 plus added grit, for instance), or regular feeding if grown in a loam-free medium. But avoid over-feeding, as with a high nitrogen fertiliser, for instance, which can cause crests to split. A pH of around 6.5 (i.e. just on the acid side of neutral) seems to suit most, and high alkalinity is to be avoided.

Watering and Feeding

Some remarkably contradictory advice has been offered in print regarding watering and feeding, particularly of cristates. This results from failure to appreciate the growth cycle from birth to senescence that calls for different treatments at different stages. When a crest first develops, it requires a big nu-

CREATING A CHIMERA

Fig. 290 (Left) A seedling graft of *Copiapoa laui* has died back to a thin skin over the *Echinopsis* stock, which is growing up through it. (GR)

Fig. 291 (Right) The emerging *Echinopsis* has been shorn of all exposed areoles to encourage growth from the junction with *Copiapoa*. See pp. 100-101 for the birth of a new chimera through a similar conjuring trick. (GR)

tritional boost if the fan is to expand and achieve its full glory. A check of any sort, as from drought or becoming potbound and starved, may be irreversible, and when subsequent growth is resumed it may revert to normal, if new crests do not emerge. In later years, when the plant body has expanded as far as the root system will allow, growth slows down and no amount of force-feeding has any effect other than to cause it to bloat, split and rot. This is the stage at which efforts should be made to propagate it for a new beginning, if this has not been done already.

This apart, the watering and feeding ritual does not differ from that for normal succulents.

Pest problems

Teratophytes are subject to the same pests and diseases as their normal antecedents but, because they have not been submitted to natural selection in the wild, they may be more vulnerable. Slugs and snails revel in the tender juicy expanses of some cristates, just as mealy bugs find readymade living quarters in the pleats and folds of others. Aphids welcome the soft new growth of some variegates, and decay bacteria and fungi gain entry through cracks and tears in oversized crests. But do not despair: the casualty rate should be no worse than for normal succulents given watchfulness and quick action when trouble brews. Systemic insecticides are ideal for destroying sap-suckers and may be the only way to clean up a large bug-ridden crest. Slug bait controls slugs and snails, and as a precaution I hang up pots of vulnerable treasures so that the attackers cannot reach them.

Once a plant has begun to rot, quick and drastic action may still not stop total collapse. By the time the soft dark patches are seen the enemy forces may be already circulating in the sap stream. Every trace of discoloured tissue should be cut away and the cut surfaces allowed to form a protective callus. If the root system has gone, this may mean treating the whole plant as a cutting. If only stem tips remain unaffected, it may be possible to save them by grafting. Remember that a phalangial crest has a long continuous meristem, and only a tiny wedge is needed to start off a new fan. Nurserymen up in the art can make many grafts from a single "one-off" cristate.

Pest control is a complex and everchanging subject, and the strategies available are best summarised as follows:

> 1. **HAND-PICKING**
>   For isolated outbreaks; mealy bugs and larger herbivores; slugs and snails after dark.
>
> 2. **TRAPS**
>   A *Inanimate*   Mousetraps; adhesive strips to catch sciara flies.
>   B *Living*   Pinguicula, Drosera and other flesh-eating plants (See *Brit.Cact.Succ.J.* 20: 80, 2002)
>
> 3. **CHEMICAL CONTROL**
>   A *Fumigation*
>   B *Contact Pesticides*, acting externally.
>   C *Systemic Pesticides*, acting internally through plant sap.
>
> 4. **BIOLOGICAL CONTROL**
>   Introduced living predators. Works best in large glasshouses where balance can be struck; pests never 100% eliminated.

Propagation: the road to Teratopia

Just about all the succulent teratophytes offered by nurseries will be clones, that is, vegetative propagations from one (rarely more) original maverick specimens. The most vigorous and stable may be from cuttings of branches (*Opuntia imbricata* 'Cristata', *Cereus* 'Abnormis', *Euphorbia lactea* 'Cristata') or from offsets (*Echeveria* crests, *Aeonium* 'Ballerina') or suckers (*Sansevieria* and *Agave* variegates). Other means are open. Old large clumps of *Pachypodium lamerei* 'Curlycrest' root down and layer themselves when lying flat on the soil and I have removed slices and grown them on. Leaf cuttings are rarely successful for variegates as these are chimerical and the green component dominates so that the striping is lost. Chahinian (1993) notes that *Sansevieria* 'Silver Hahnii' comes true from leaf cuttings, but the similar-looking 'Moonshine' does not. Leaves from crest-prone echeverias occasionally regenerate the crest, but the experiment is of more academic than practical value.

Seed raising from teratophytes is a voyage into the unknown. For reasons already made clear, even if viable seed is set you can rarely expect it to self-perpetuate, let alone breed true. But few seed-raisers can resist the urge to try if and when seed is available, and may be in for surprises. Seed from a cristate *Echinopsis* gave just 3% of fasciated seedlings; for cristate *Gymnocalycium mihanovichii*, however, 30% of the seedlings are said to develop crests. *Echinopsis chamaecereus* 'Crassicaulis Cristata' has already been mentioned as the unique example of a succulent breeding true for fasciation.

Grafting

Grafting is the safe and sure way to preserve rarities or rescue bits of them if they have collapsed with rot. It is possible in all the major groups of dicot stem succulents, and some leaf succulents, but not in monocots, although there are a few claims of limited success there too. For some reason grafting has until recently been little practised outside of Cactaceae, with very few euphorbias and stapeliads, but experiments show that many other families containing succulents are amenable to grafting and some (as *Pachypodium*) are even easier to work with than cacti. Choice of rootstock is less critical in some families than in others. Cacti seem most obliging, and one can get fully successful unions from species belonging to different subfamilies, as *Disocactus* on *Opuntia* or just about anything on *Pereskiopsis*. Euphorbias, on the other hand, are rather more choosy (Horwood 1983), and one has to cope with the white poisonous latex which exudes from both cut surfaces. It can be washed off with a jet of water, or you can leave it to bleed for a minute and then slice a piece from the surface; the area below will be almost clear.

As a guide for would-be grafters, I list below a personal choice of favourite rootstocks for normal as well as teratological succulents.

Recommended Grafting Stocks

Cactaceae

Echinopsis pachanoi	Easy to handle
Echinopsis spachiana	Very (too?) vigorous
Echinopsis multiplex or allies	Good but offset too much
Harrisia bonplandii	Slender-stemmed
Selenicereus spinulosus	Slender-stemmed
Opuntia ficus-indica, monacantha, robusta, etc.	For other dwarf opuntias mainly
Pereskiopsis porteri	Ideal for tiny seedlings

Myrtillocactus geometrizans and *Hylocereus undatus*, favoured in Japan, are tender and usually short-lived in Europe

Euphorbiaceae

Euphorbia obesa best for dwarf treasures, *E. suzannae* and *E. obesa* cristates
Euphorbia fruticosa similar but offsets freely
Euphorbia mammillaris tends to be short-lived
Euphorbia canariensis is favoured by some

Crassulaceae

Rarely needed, but arborescent *Crassula ovata* would be a first choice

Apocynaceae

Pachypodium lamerei seems ideal for all *Pachypodium* species; *Nerium* (oleander) has been used for *Adenium*

Asclepiadaceae

Ceropegia linearis ssp. *woodii* tubers
Stapelia gigantea

Portulacaceae

Portulacaria afra suits *Ceraria* species well

Didiereaceae

Alluaudia procera seems ideal, and offsets root readily in the hotbox

Compositae (Asteraceae)

Senecio ficoides is hugely vigorous and easy to work with crested senecios

---

For scions containing at least some green tissue, the grafting stock can be kept short and hidden by rocks, if desired, to avoid the artificial "lollipop look" of a ball on top of a long thin stock. For albinos it is important to realise that the green tissue of the stock provides their food supply, so one should ensure that the stock is large enough and renewed as soon as it starts to age and cork over.

Seedling grafting was pioneered in Japan as a means of saving newly germinated cacti lacking chlorophyll. For this you need rooted cuttings of *Pereskiopsis*, a truly remarkable Mexican shrub. I collected mine, *P. porteri* (GR534), from a thicket south-east of Triunfo in Baja California in 1974 in the form of one tiny cutting and soon learned that the price of all its virtues as the perfect stock was the glochids: almost invisible barbed spines deep within each areole that make it virtually impossible to handle. However, this is easily overcome by the use of blunt-ended forceps, steel or plastic, with the jaws tipped with a short length of rubber or plastic tubing if you want to lessen the risk of bruising the soft sappy stem. Such cuttings root rapidly in the hotbox - heat is the key to success here - and can be potted singly: I favour square pots which stack together easily. You will need good eyesight (or a magnifier on a stand), a razor blade or scalpel and a steady hand. The smallest seedlings I have done were about 2 mm in diameter. The tip of the *Pereskiopsis* is sliced off first, steadying it with the aforementioned forceps. Then the seedling is bisected and the top half transferred while still on the knife to slide into place on the stock. A gentle press with a finger tip will ensure that it makes contact and squeeze out any bubbles of air.

Cultivation

GRAFTED CRISTATE CACTI

Note the scion centrally placed to match the vascular ring of the stock.

Opposite page:

Fig. 292 (Above) *Cleistocactus* sp. Fasciation can conceal the identity of familiar species. (SD)

Fig. 293 (Below) *Pilosocereus* sp. with the short stock discreetly hidden. (SD)

Fig. 294 (Above) *Turbinicarpus lophophoroides.* (SD)

Fig. 295 (Right) *Mammillaria deherdtiana* monstrose grafted on *Echinopsis*. (HB)

Usually the gummy sap of cacti is enough to hold it in place, but the simplest way of adding pressure is by finding a glass specimen tube of the right size and inverting it over the graft, having snipped away any leaves that get in the way. Gadgeteers may devise adjustable stands with leaf springs and a tiny cube of sponge plastic on top of the scion, or you can loop an elastic band round the whole as for grafts of larger plants. The pot is then returned to the propagator and kept well-watered and fed. Within a few days one should be able to see if all is well; if not one can always slice the top off and start again. *Pereskiopsis* is ideal for pumping up tiny crests in double-quick time, but a more permanent, thicker stock may be required later to avoid bloating, or when the green starts to cork over if the scion is an albino.

Teratomania–the quest for new monsters

You do not have to travel thousands of miles and tangle with the law to collect new teratophytes. Some can be born in seedpans or on shoot tips of plants in your own glasshouse. There is something uniquely satisfying in picking through a pan of seedlings, and saving just one odd miscreant that most growers would have instinctively discarded. An equal thrill is exploring the thousands of potted seedlings in a large nursery and choosing one oddball, hoping that the vendor doesn't spot the yellow streak or broadening apex and hastily withdraw it from sale. Mutant branches on adult plants can be cut off and rooted or grafted in one's own collection. They turn up when least expected and often on the most unlikely plants. In time one learns to know what to look for, and whether or not it is likely to merit the effort to propagate it. Hybrids, being an unbalanced mixture of two sets of chromosomes, seem especially prone to mutate.

Chimeras are all more or less prone to throw shoots of one component or another. The *Crassula* in Fig. 500 has sported an all-yellow branch from the upper component of the mix; if the core component broke out we would see it as all-green like the parent species. Chahinian (1999) has plotted the possible mutations within three-layered periclinal chimeras by duplication or deletion of individual layers. For *Sansevieria trifasciata* cultivars frequent jumps are as follows (see p. 93):

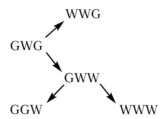

Commonest involves a reversal of layers, so that an edge stripe becomes a midstripe with green edges, or vice versa. He gives advice on how to detect spontaneous mutants in a *Sansevieria* collection, by holding the young leaves against a strong light source to reveal the contrast between two areas of colour.

> *"And the moral of that is –"*
> – the Duchess in Alice in Wonderland,
> Chapter 9

For succulents the future lies in propagation. Master the art of rooting cuttings and grafting and you will be able to preserve rarities and multiply them to exchange with other collectors. Master the art of seed raising and sooner or later you will be picking out crests and variegates of your very own - each unique and perhaps eventually meriting a cultivar name and distribution through nurseries. You may not become rich, but the satisfaction of achievement is reward enough. And here is something to cheer you on: it is reported that 1 in 200,000 seedlings of *Carnegiea gigantea* comes up cristate, but in *Pachypodium lamerei* 1 in 1,000 is cristate or variegated!

Speculations, Tests and Deductions

The subjects of this book all invite the same questions when one confronts them for the first time. What is going on? Why did it happen? What caused it? The last is the least answerable at present, but

Cultivation

at least the first is open to experiments, some requiring laboratory and microscope facilities, some within the reach of dedicated amateurs. It must be stressed that although a large body of scientific analysis exists (Tilney-Bassett 1986), most of it involves plants other than succulents, and some of the assignments to set categories in this book are the result of guesses by analogy rather than actual tests.

It is easy to dub any anomalous growth as "a mutation", or "physiological disorder" and leave it at that. Can one be more precise? Here are some guide-lines to assist diagnosis. Further help in sorting out different races of 3-layered chimeras has already been given on p. 95.

1) Cultural disorders

Unpot the plant, check the roots, give it fresh soil and pamper it in conditions known to favour growth, avoiding too much shade or sun. If it reverts to normal in colouring and growth pattern you can put down any previous symptoms to accident or bad cultivation.

2) Root and leaf cutting tests for suspected chimeras

Adventitious roots arise from deep within the stem and carry only the core component (Fig. 296). Many plants with fleshy roots can be raised from cuttings of these (e.g. *Pachypodium succulentum*). Thus a WWG or WGG (p. 93) chimera raised from root cuttings will be all-green, as in the core component.

With leaf cuttings the new meristem can arise from anywhere on the surface, but most commonly from green tissue. In a genuine chimera only very rarely will the original variegation pattern be reproduced. One can say with conviction that a variegated plant that comes true from leaf cuttings is not of the chimerical type.

3) Grafting as a test for pathogens

A proliferous cactus, such as the *Opuntia* shown in Fig. 227, has been shown to transmit the effect across a graft. Micro-organisms responsible travel in the sapstream of the plant. Intergrafting variegated and all-green plants gives a means of testing if a virus is responsible or not. In *Pachypodium*, even single variegated leaves can be grafted and the sticky sap holds them in place while they unite.

4) Testing heritability

The germ line, that is, the cells that ultimately form gametes and seeds, have their origin in the middle layer of a meristem, not in the skin tissues. Thus a chimera can breed from only one of its components, that below the surface. A few exceptions are known (Tilney-Bassett 1986: 59), but raising seedlings remains one of the most useful tests of a suspected chimera. It also could bring to light rare cases of inherited ability to fasciate.

5) Mutilation

Removing all the growing points from a suspected chimera can force the plant to break out from deep within the stem at an exposed surface and reveal the core component of a chimera. Unidentified cristates can also be identified if normal shoots can similarly be persuaded to arise away from the crest.

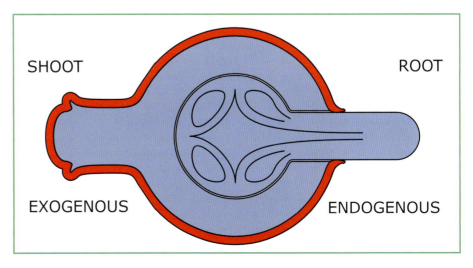

Fig. 296 Endogenous origin af a root. Because roots arise from deep within a stem, they are made up of the core component only.

Interlude E

Captive Crests

Teratophytes have a minimal chance of survival in the wild. Many never flower, and most are less competitive than their normal parents. In cultivation we can preserve them, grow them larger and finer and, in many cases, propagate them so that their unique beauty and sculptural perfection can be admired among plant lovers everywhere. This interlude looks at pot plants. Many of the cacti are grafted, although ideally, as with garden roses, the stock is kept short and becomes hidden as the crest grows.

Captive Crests

Fig. 297 (Above) *Stenocactus crispatus* (HM)

Fig. 298 (Below) *Mammillaria hernandezii* (SD)

Captive Crests

Opposite page:

Fig. 299 (Above) Broadening seedling of *Euphorbia obesa*. (SR)

Fig. 300 (Below) *Orbea ciliata*, prone to ring-cristation. (HM)

Fig. 301 (Right) *Echeveria coccinea* 'Furry Fan', said to come true from leaves by Harry Mak. (HM)

Fig. 302 (Below) x *Cremneria expatriata*, a bigener combining genes of *Cremnophila* and *Echeveria*, and losing control. (HM)

Fig. 303 (Above) *Echinopsis backebergii* (SD)
Fig. 304 (Below) *Myrtillocactus eichlamii* (SD)

Captive Crests

Fig. 305 (Above) *Parodia magnifica* (?) (WW)

Fig. 306 (Below) *Parodia werneri* (WW)

Fig. 307 (Left)
Rebutia einsteinii var. *gonjianii* (WW)

Fig. 308 (Below)
Rebutia canigueralii
(*Sulcorebutia rauschii*)
(WW)

Opposite page:

Fig. 309 (Above)
Mammillaria longiflora
(HM)

Fig. 310 (Below)
Mammillaria zeilmanniana
(HM)

Captive Crests

Fig. 311 (Above) An unidentified *Eriosyce* (*Neoporteria*). (PC)

Fig. 312 (Below) *Rebutia heliosa* freaking out. (SP)

The appeal of Teratophytes

chapter 9

Even some of those who make succulents their chosen favourites among decorative plants draw the line at including crests, variegates and other departures from the approved norm (grafts are also included in the ban). They give good reasons for their disapproval: there are enough desirable wild species already without pandering to the taste for freaks. In any case, some of the examples look diseased, tumorous or just downright ugly. Even confirmation that most teratophytes are not diseased (a few virus-induced variegates being one exception) does little to convert the opposition. Yet at the outset there are conflicts of interest. We wholeheartedly deplore malformation in the Animal Kingdom but condone it in many favourite plants: double roses, giant seedless fruits and cauliflowers.

Indeed, the study of teratophytes has to take into account human idiosyncrasies, among which the urge to seek out and collect any sort of novelty comes to the fore. We see it in action in many ways. Early explorers naturally sought anything that looked different from the common crowd. What they brought back, living or pressed, probably represented the extremes: the largest, dwarfest, most colourful and appealing. If these are described as new, we get a false impression of the variation of species in the wild. The middle-of-the-range majority have been overlooked. In early days, plants we now know to be teratological were often dignified with latinised names: Salm-Dyck's *Cactus abnormis* (*Cereus abnormis* Sweet; Fig. 260) and *Sansevieria laurentii* De Wild. (Fig. 186). Such entities were a problem to fit within Linnaeus's binomial system, but nowadays we have an International Code of Nomenclature for Cultivated Plants (ICNCP), and treat these as cultivars: *Cereus* 'Abnormis' and *Sansevieria trifasciata* 'Laurentii'.

In *A History of Succulent Plants* I rashly devoted a chapter to aesthetics and attempted to analyse just what it is about succulents that catches the eye and turns some otherwise normal folk into goggling obsessives. Since I have not been pilloried for this by enraged artists or aesthetes I assume that it has at least a grain of truth in it. Succulents are unique for their stark geometry, their high level of symmetry and their bold prime colours. Emotionally they suggest solidity, durability, implacability, the utmost economy of means and survival against all odds. Teratophytes of the type figured in this book share all these features but with departures on two fronts: symmetry and coloration.

Cristate stem succulents lose their radial symmetry, and monstrose examples are even less regular: they can appear quite amorphous. But just as some people prefer the billowy contours of oaks and willows to the stiffly conical conifers, so the protean shapes of the foregoing take on a new aspect to win admiration. Unpredictability is the attractant: on a nurseryman's show bench no two will be exactly alike.

As for colours, it is the variegates that break up the monotony of washes of a single shade with their stripes, splashes and spots of another colour, and this is welcomed by some as adding variety and overall appeal to a collection.

The thirst for novelty among our decorative plants is matched by their seemingly endless outpouring, as genes reshuffle, mutate and are selected out and allowed to survive under entirely artificial conditions of nurture in our glasshouses. Every digression from normal growth is likely to come under the spotlight and be perpetuated as cuttings or grafts. This book has covered only a sampling of the more striking and horticulturally desirable types. Much has been left out, especially items which, however miraculous and offbeat, are unstable or unpropagatable. A wider field could have encompassed other phenomena, such as hormonal mix-ups when cactus fruits revert into vegetative shoots, or the weird amalgam of aloe leaves and inflorescences featured in *Alsterworthia* 2: 17-19, 2002. For the teratophile on the hunt there is truly no limit to what he might come across.

Interlude F

Showpieces

A specialist collection of succulent teratophytes is indeed a sight to remember. It attracts artists who respond to the provocative contours and colours. It stimulates photographers in search of novel three-dimensional subjects for the camera. It tantalises botanists who have to rethink the rules to try to explain them. And it brings lasting joy to the collector who knows that there is no end to the choice of future additions or to the unexpected turns that they may take. Given more such collections, we could have a new cult in the making!

Showpieces

Figs. 313-315 (Above) A remarkable assemblage of teratophytes collected by Harry Mak. (HM)

Fig. 316 (Right) Cristates in the De Herdt nursery. (GR)

Showpieces

Opposite page:

SHOWS

Figs. 317, 318 (Upper left and lower left) Cristates at a BCSS show. (GR)

Fig. 319 (Lower right) Variegates on the showbench in San Diego. (SR)

SCULPTURES

Fig. 320 (Right) *Myrtillocactus geometrizans* crest. (HM)

Fig. 321 (Below) *Espostoa ritteri* crest. Most espostoas are known to fasciate, and propagations like this graft are justly popular for the mane of white hair. (GR)

Showpieces

SCULPTURES CTD.

Opposite page:

Fig. 322 (Above) *Aztekium ritteri* crest. (SR)

Fig. 323 (Below) *Mammillaria bocasana* 'Fred' looking unrecognisable in this bizarre crest. (SD)

Fig. 324 (Above) "Henry Moore's +*Hylogymnocalycium*"? (HM)

Fig. 325 (Right) *Senecio stapeliiformis* ssp. *minor* 'Panoply', repetitive cristate, a superb living sculpture. (GR)

SCULPTURES CTD.

Fig. 326 (Above) *Euphorbia* x *bothae* 'Needle Hills'. (HM)

Fig. 327 (Below) Cristate *Sinocrassula yunnanensis*. (GR)

Showpieces

Fig. 328 (Above) *Euphorbia neriifolia* crest. (HM)

Fig. 329 (Below) *Crassula muscosa* crests. (HM)

Showpieces

SCULPTURES CTD.

Opposite page:

Fig. 330 (Above) *Haworthia cymbiformis* var. *obtusa* 'Chik-chun Mak'. (HM)

Fig. 331 (Below) *Kalanchoe* 'Pink Butterflies'. (HM)

Fig. 332 (Right) *Sedum pachyphyllum* 'Multifingers'. (HM)

Fig. 333 (Below) *Sedum praealtum* 'Jade Fan'. (HM)

Classified Odds
chapter 10

A systematic sampling of succulent teratophytes arranged under Family

The subjects of this book turn up, often when least expected, scattered among all the Families that have evolved succulence, though unequally and erratically distributed. Some Families keep to the straight and narrow path and hardly ever let a gene slip: the Aizoaceae (Mesembryanthemum Family) for example. The Cactaceae score ten out of ten for the diversity and extravagance of their fasciations and monstrosities, but far fewer points for variegation. The big monocot Families including *Agave* and *Aloe* respectively score almost zero for cristates, but highest of all for spectacular displays of leaf striping.

No attempt is made here to give complete coverage in pictures or even in a name list: it would be never-ending, and during compilation some would become extinct while other novelties were still coming to light. Instead, the reader can have the pleasure of saying: "Oh, I've got one that isn't in Rowley's book...!" and mentally sticking in the pot a new price tag three times the previous valuation.

In absence of a more obvious system of classification I begin with the stem succulents most prone to fasciate and go on to leaf succulents via Crassulaceae which is rich in both crests and variegates. Readers will probably thank me in that there are no Latin diagnoses, citations of type specimens, unpronounceable place names, maps or geological data; just plants, plants and more beautiful plants!

Cactaceae, the Cactus Family

Cristates

Cacti excel in fasciation in all its protean guises; they have outsize meristems and the fatter and softer the stems, the more striking are the growth aberrations. They range from the largest of all succulent cristates in *Carnegiea* (Figs. 5, 342-345), and *Ferocactus* (Figs. 6, 364) down to tiny miniatures ideal for growers short of space who put quality before size (Fig. 397). Salm-Dyck's fine painting of a monstrose cereus (Fig. 260) shows that such freak growths were esteemed as early as 1805, and he also figured a *Stenocereus griseus* with a slightly spiralled stem tip.

Catalogues have been drawn up of cacti known to sport teratologies. Shurly (1959: 86–87) lists names of 224 cacti known as crests, combining lists previously published in *Cactus (Belgium)* **9**: 59–61, 1939 and *Cact.Succ.J.(U.S.)* **12**: 109, 1940. Hirose & Yokoi (1998) illustrate 28 cacti showing variegation in the genera *Ariocarpus* (2), *Astrophytum* (3), *Aztekium* (1), *Cereus* (1), *Coryphantha* (3), *Gymnocalycium* (1), *Echinopsis* (2), *Lophophora* (1), *Mammillaria* (2), *Obregonia* (1), *Oreocereus* (1), *Parodia* (1), *Pereskia* (2), *Pereskiopsis* (1), *Rebutia* (2), *Schlumbergera* (1), *Stenocactus* (1), *Stenocereus* (1) and *Uebelmannia* (1).

But such lists serve little purpose and are soon out of date: no sooner is *Geohintonia* smuggled into Europe than the news breaks that somebody has a cristate seedling (Figs. 367, 368). One is left wondering if any cactus is immune! The pictures selected here are but a few of what is available, but give a fair sampling of the sizes and patterns adopted. Judicious pruning of the larger types can result in spectacular sculptural effects. Notable absentees are any of the thin-stemmed epiphytes (forest cacti; Tribes Hylocereae and Rhipsalideae). I once had an attractive cristate epicactus that looked like parsley covered with white whiskers, but have seen no example in wild species (Uitewaal 1959).

It should be mentioned that some globular cacti, large or small, with broad flat apices habitually expand in old age to form a linear or even starlike apex (Figs. 43, 44). This resembles fasciation, but in most cases never expands into a fan, and is regarded as normal.

Figs. 334, 335 (Above and below) *Ariocarpus kotschoubeyanus* with buds aligned along the crest opening to one long bouquet. (WW)

Figs. 336, 337 *Ariocarpus retusus* crests in the Huntington Botanic Garden (above) and (below) in Stuart Riley's collection. (SR)

Fig. 338 (Above) *Ariocarpus retusus* ssp. *trigonus* cristate with 3 normal specimens, highly valued by collectors, and wild examples were rarely left undug. (GR)

Fig. 339 (Below) *Astrophytum myriostigma* cristate. The normal plant has a single unbranched head and five ribs. (GR)

Fig. 340 (Left) *Astrophytum myriostigma* cristate in a show in San Diego. (SR)

Fig. 341 (Below) *Blossfeldia liliputana* - a good example of repetitive cristation affecting every head. (BH)

Opposite page:

Figs. 342-344 *Carnegiea gigantea* crests; largest and most celebrated of all fasciated cacti, and a talking point whenever encountered. No two are alike. (GR)

Cactaceae - Cristates

Fig. 345 Another saguaro that continually changes its mind. (GR)

Cactaceae - Cristates

Fig. 346 (Above) Part of Doug Donaldson's collection of *Astrophytum* cvs. (GR)

Fig. 347 (Right) *Cereus spegazzinii* (*Monvillea marmorata*) 'Cristatus' needs topiary to encourage a good shape and remove reversions. (GR)

Fig. 348 (Below) *Cephalocereus senilis* crest. (SD)

Fig. 349 (Above left) *Cleistocactus ritteri* cristate – a particularly handsome sculptural effect with three fans. (GR)

Fig. 350 (Above right) *Coryphantha recurvata*: a large old clump with some of the heads fasciated. (GR)

Fig. 351 (Below) *Cleistocactus strausii* crest at the cerebroid or cerebriform stage. (SR)

Fig. 352 (Above left) *Copiapoa tenuissima*. (SD)

Fig. 353 (Above right) *Discocactus horstii* is so popular for its compact form and white, scented nocturnal flowers that a chance cristate would never pass unnoticed. Grafting is essential. (GR)

Fig. 354 (Below) Cristate seedling of the golden barrel cactus, *Echinocactus grusonii*. (GR)

Fig. 355 (Left) Three crested specimens of *Echinocactus grusonii* yellow, white and spineless in a Dutch collection. (SR)

Fig. 356 (Middle) *Echinocactus grusonii* - a near-spineless crest in close-up. (SR)

Fig. 357 (Bottom) *Echinocereus knippelianus* crest. (HM)

Fig. 358 (Above left)
Echinocereus brandegei cristate. (JP)

Fig. 359 (Above right)
Echinocereus coccineus cristate, showing the beautifully symmetrical, vigorous growth produced by grafting. (JP)

Fig. 360 (Right)
Echinocereus viridiflorus ssp. *chloranthus* crest GR608 began as a single tiny wedge-shaped offset on a large old plant I found in Soledad Canyon, Organ Mountains, New Mexico. It grew well on its own roots and never reverted. (GR)

Fig. 361 (Below)
Echinocereus russanthus crest showing the serpentine folding that takes place as a flattened stem enlarges more at the top than at the bottom. (GR)

Fig. 362 (Top left) Crests of *Echinocereus* (*Wilcoxia*) sp. (SR)

Fig. 363 (Above) *Echinopsis chamaecereus* 'Crassicaulis Cristata': another view (cf. Fig. 83) with a cristate flower and others normal. (GR)

Fig. 364 (Above right) Crests are uncommon in the larger barrel cacti, and one can only guess at the age of this massive *Ferocactus wislizeni*. (GR)

Fig. 365 (Above) Another cristate *F. wislizeni* coming into bloom from normal areoles either side of the phalangial apex. (GR)

Fig. 366 (Below) Abundant yellow fruits on a cristate *Ferocactus wislizeni*. Flowers, fruits and seeds are exactly as on normal plants. (JH)

Cactaceae - Cristates

Opposite page:

Fig. 367 (Above left) *Geohintonia mexicana*: a crest from a normal offset. (FXS)

Fig. 368 (Above right) *Geohintonia mexicana*: graft from a cristate seedling. (FXS)

Fig. 369 (Below) *Gymnocalycium mihanovichii* cristate. (WW)

Fig. 370 (Right) *Haageocereus pseudomelanostele* (*multangularis*). (GR)

Fig. 371 (Below) *Haageocereus* (*Weberbauerocereus*) *weberbaueri* cristate seen from above. (GR)

Fig. 372 (Top left) *Mammillaria bocasana* 'Multilanata Crest' has recently become popular with its exceptional snow-white armature and easy, vigorous growth on its own roots. (GR)

Fig. 373 (Middle left) *Mammillaria duwei*, a fine crested specimen but a target for mealy bugs amid the pleats and folds. (JP)

Fig. 374 (Bottom left) *Mammillaria elegans* crest. (HM)

Fig. 375 (Bottom right) *Mammillaria carmenae* cristate, almost hiding its grafting stock. (JP)

Opposite page:

Fig. 376 (Top left) *Mammillaria elongata* cristate: vigorous, tough and undemanding in cultivation. (JP)

Fig. 377 (Top right) *Mammillaria hahniana* ssp. *woodsii*. (HM)

Fig. 378 (Middle left) *Mammillaria lasiacantha* ssp. *egregia*. (HM)

Fig. 379 (Middle right) *Mammillaria nunezii* ssp. *bella*. (WW)

Fig. 380 (Bottom left) *Mammillaria schiedeana* var. *plumosa*. (JP)

Fig. 381 (Bottom right) *Mammillaria spinosissima* crest. (HM)

Cactaceae - Cristates

Fig. 382 (Above) *Mammillaria* crests are legion, although few survive for long enough to grow into such splendid snake-like coils as this *M. supertexta*. (GR)

Fig. 383 (Below) *Mammillaria theresae* variations in Stuart Riley's collection. (SR)

Fig. 384 (Above) *Mammillaria wildii* 'Cristata' mass-produced in a nursery in Fresno, California. (GR)
Fig. 385 (Below) *Mammillaria spinosissima* 'Crested Pico'. (HM)

Fig. 386 *Obregonia denegrii* crest. (JN)

Fig. 387 (Above) *Opuntia lanceolata* crests. (HM)

Fig. 388 (Below) *Opuntia erectoclada*, two cristate shoots. Detached and rooted, they produced only normal shoots. (GR)

Fig. 389 (Left) *Oreocereus celsianus* crest. (SR)

Fig. 390 (Below left) *Pachycereus marginatus* cristate in a nursery in the Netherlands. (GR) & 391 (Below right) a smaller plant of the same. (SR)

Fig. 392 (Bottom right) *Pachycereus pringlei* cristate; uncommon and slow growing. (GR)

Fig. 393 (Right)
Parodia (*Notocactus*)
buiningii seedling crest. (SR)

Fig. 394 (Below right)
Parodia 'Mirabilis'
(the name seems to be
unofficial) with two normal
heads peeping out from
a superb writhing mound
of cristation. (GR)

Fig. 395 (Bottom left)
Parodia (*Notocactus*)
leninghausii 'Cristata',
grafted. In general,
the larger the stock the
faster the scion will grow.
(GR)

Fig. 396 (Bottom right)
Parodia (*Notocactus*)
scopa cristate. (WW)

Fig. 397 (Top) *Rebutia canigueralii* (*Sulcorebutia rauschii*) – a cristate for all ages. But beware of mealy bug in the nooks and crannies! (GR)

Fig. 398 (Centre) *Pilosocereus lanuginosus (tillianus)*, another typical bifacial phalangial crest. (JP)

Fig. 399 (Bottom) *Pilosocereus bradei* cristate. (JP)

Opposite page:

Fig. 400 (Above) *Rebutia steinbachii* ssp. *tiraquensis* cristate. (HM)

Fig. 401 (Below) *Stenocactus vaupelianus* at Cante. (WW)

Cactaceae - Cristates

Fig. 402 (Above) *Stenocereus eruca* crest. (SR)

Fig. 403 (Below) *Turbinicarpus pseudopectinatus* cristate – one of many show plants in the fine collection of Doris Sharp in Reading. (GR)

Fig. 404 (Above) *Uebelmannia pectinifera* ssp. *flavispina*: a remarkable twin crest coming from a single root. (GR)

Fig. 405 (Below) The dividing line between fasciation and monstrosity if often blurred. This *Mammillaria painteri* shows bits of both. (GR)

Variegates

Salm-Dyck is also the pioneer in figuring variegated cacti (see p. 65), although his *Hylocereus* cultivar with overall yellow glow is now thought to be extinct. It typifies the fairly stable WG type of chimera in which the pallor is uniform overall. More commonly it varies according to the relative thicknesses of the upper layers of cells, resulting in a blotchy or marbled effect. In the *Astrophytum* of Fig. 407 the variegation looks more like the work of an unstable gene that has switched off chlorophyll development in an otherwise normal seedling. But we cannot be sure, because such events are too rare to lend themselves to experimentation.

Russia's leading expert on variegated plants, Anatoly Mikhaltsov (2000) claims that there are variegates of 600 cactus species belonging to 89 genera. He has produced a classification of them into 14 groups based on presence or absence of chlorophyll, stem colour and patterning. In the summary on p. 201 I omit his Latin names for the cultivar groups as they do not accord with either of the nomenclature codes.

The polychromatic *Gymnocalycium mihanovichii* remains star of the show for covering its bodies in colours normally reserved for flowers (Figs. 127-137), and suffers only from over-familiarity and unfair rejection through ignorance of how to preserve it in captivity.

Fig. 406 (Above) *Astrophytum* variegated hybrid. (GR)

Fig. 407 (Below) *Astrophytum myriostigma* 'Nudum' – a one-off seedling with local lack of chlorophyll. Note how the pallid regions appear shrunken from weaker growth than adjacent green tissue. (GR)

Fig. 408 (Below) *Stenocactus crispatus* (variegated). (HM)

Cactaceae - Variegates

Mikhaltsov's classification of variegation patterns in Cactaceae			Epidermis colour
Plant lacking chlorophyll			1. White
			2. Pink
Plant in part deficient in chlorophyll	Stems concolorous		3. Orange
			4. Yellow
			5. Off-white
			6. Pink
			7. Red
	Stems variegated	Stems bicolour	8. White variegated
			9. Dark variegated
			10. Yellow variegated
			11. Pink variegated
			12. Red variegated
		Stems multicolour	13. Variegated
Plant with chlorophyll			14. Blackish purple

Fig. 409 *Ariocarpus retusus*, a red variant from Czechoslovakia. (SR)

Fig. 410 (Left) *Eriosyce* (*Neoporteria*) *occulta*, a red variegate. (SR)

Fig. 411 (Below left) *Gymnocalycium mihanovichii* 'Hibotan Nishiki' is justly popular for its extraordinary body colouring: not a green patch in sight! (GR)

Fig. 412 (Below right) *Ferocactus echidne*: an aberrant seedling variously marbled and spotted. Such specimens are highly prized in Japan – and easily sun-scorched. (GR)

Fig. 413 (Bottom left) *Gymnocalycium mihanovichii* - an extreme pallid variant. (SR)

Opposite page:

Fig. 414 (Upper right) *Matucana madisoniorum* variegate. (SR)

Fig. 415 (Middle right) Variegated cacti (GR) and
Fig. 416 (Lower right) *Gymnocalycium mihanovichii* variegates - both in the nursery of Doug Donaldson. (GR)

Cactaceae - Variegates

Euphorbiaceae, the Spurge Family

The spurge family in Africa produces a diversity of cristations in parallel to those in American cacti, and its occasional variegates are generally better patterned. As in Cactaceae, some, such as the crested branches of shrubs and trees, are usually grown from cuttings on their own roots. Crests of the dwarf, spherical species are a different proposition, and more challenging to multiply from wedge grafts. The sumptuous *Euphorbia Journal* includes many fine pictures of fasciated euphorbias, notably in the articles by Rauh (1988) and Hunter (1988). Beginner's choice here would be *E. lactea* 'Cristata', in commerce as rooted cuttings that grow rapidly and eventually form grotesque squirming mounds of greenery up to a metre across.

Of the variegated succulent euphorbias, *E. lactea* again stands out with a virtuoso performance (Fig. 440) giving the aptly named 'White Ghost' (sometimes less flatteringly offered as 'Grey Ghost'). Equally startling is *E. trigona* 'Red Ghost'. Both grow well on their own roots, so must have plenty of chlorophyll beneath all that make-up. A cristate variant of 'White Ghost' goes under the name 'Spring Horse' in Japan (Fig. 428). Equally suited for the beginner is the dapper *E. submammillaris* 'Indian Corn' (Fig. 441), and if size is all important the strikingly yellow-splashed variant of *E. abyssinica* (*ammak*) will soon make its presence felt (Fig. 439). *E. suzannae* is especially interesting, as has already been noted, for its unstable gene producing whole blocks of white, apparently at random, and for combining this with fasciation in the even more remarkable 'Maelstrom' (Fig. 444). There is in addition a cristate of the all-green plant.

A few cultivars from genera other than *Euphorbia* deserve mention here. *Pedilanthus tithymaloides* has several variants with attractively variegated foliage (Fig. 448), and *P. macrocarpus* is prone to fasciate at branch tips (Fig. 447). The *Euphorbia Journal* **5** p.20 has an arresting picture by Ron LaFon of an extravagantly fasciated shoot of *Jatropha dioica*.

CRISTATES

Fig. 417 (Left) Cristate euphorbias in Keith Mortimer's collection in 1967. *E. ledienii* (rear left); *E.* sp? (rear right); *E. suzannae*, *E. woodii* and *E. obesa* (front row). (GR)

Fig. 418 (Below) *E. bussei* var. *kibwezensis* cristate. (HM)

Opposite page:

Fig. 419 (Above) An exceptionally fine cristate development in *E. bussei* var. *kibwezensis*. (GR)

Fig. 420 (Below) Cresting *Euphorbia officinarum*, Oued Massa. (BJ)

Euphorbiaceae - Cristates

Fig. 421 (Above) *Euphorbia flanaganii* with a phalangial crest for the main stem. (HM)

Fig. 422 (Below) *Euphorbia flanaganii* even more extravagantly fasciated. (RS)

Fig. 423 (Above left) *Euphorbia flanaganii* branch crest. (HM)

Fig. 424 (Above right) *Euphorbia lactea* 'Spring Horse', variegated as well as cristate. The significance of the Japanese name escapes me. (GR)

Fig. 425 (Below) *Euphorbia gummifera* with crested branches, photographed by Graham Williamson. (GW)

Fig. 426 (Above) *Euphorbia hallii* crested; note the abundant evidence of flowering. (LN)

Fig. 427 (Below) *Euphorbia horrida* cristate. (SD)

Fig. 428 (Above) *Euphorbia lactea* 'Spring Horse', John Pilbeam's fine specimen. (JP)

Fig. 429 (Below) *Euphorbia mammillaris* cristate. (GW)

Fig. 430 (Above) *Euphorbia milii* var. *longifolia* cristate. (WR)

Fig. 431 (Below) *Euphorbia neriifolia* cristate. (HM)

Fig. 432 (Above) *Euphorbia neriifolia* cristate in St Petersburg Botanical Garden. (VG)

Fig. 433 (Below) *Euphorbia obesa* 'Rocky Mountain', a real collector's piece and sculptural beauty. (SD)

Fig. 434 (Left) Another *E. obesa* 'Cristata'. It is usually to be seen grafted. Here a crest on its own roots has grown almost full circle. (GR)

Fig. 435 (Below) *Euphorbia ramiglans* in habitat with occasional crests. (GW)

Opposite page:

Fig. 436 (Above) The "fish-scale" spurge, *Euphorbia piscidermis*, adds to its uniqueness by sometimes going two-headed or cristate. These two crests arose from a single small scion that lost its growing point in my own glasshouse. (GR)

Fig. 437 (Centre) *E. resinifera*: a single crest found in Morocco and brought back by J. Natsoulas. (GR)

Fig. 438 (Below) *E. turbiniformis* crest among Frank Horwood's treasures at Abbey Garden. (GR)

Euphorbiaceae - Cristates

VARIEGATES

Fig. 439 (Left) *Euphorbia abyssinica* 'Milky Totem'. (HM)

Fig. 440 (Below left) *E. lactea* 'White Ghost' (rear) and *E. trigona* 'Red Ghost' (centre), both as vigorous as the normal plant, which is green marbled milky white (hence the name) down the centre between ribs. (GR)

Fig. 441 (Below right) This neat and decorative cultivar, *E. submammillaris* 'Indian Corn', is stable and no less vigorous than the type. (GR)

Opposite page:

Fig. 442 (Above) *Euphorbia milii* 'Golden Crown'. (HM)

Fig. 443 (Below) *Euphorbia obesa* variegated seedling. (SR)

Euphorbiaceae - Variegates

Opposite page:

Fig. 444 (Above) Variegation in *E. suzannae* 'Maelstrom' is probably caused by an unstable gene. (HM)

Fig. 445 (Below) *Monadenium ellenbeckii* extravagantly fasciated. (LN)

Fig. 446 (Upper right) *Monadenium lugardae* with crested shoots. (LN)

Fig. 447 (Middle right) *Pedilanthus macrocarpus* is fasciation-prone as seen on several shoots here. (GR)

Fig. 448 (Lower right) *P. tithymaloides* has sported several cultivars with particoloured foliage. This one has pale yellow margins. (HM)

Asclepiadaceae, the Milkweed Family

A cristate *Orbea* (*Stapelia*) *variegata* was illustrated as early as 1700 and it became something of a cult plant, widely propagated and figured in many florilegia (White & Sloane 1937 1: 79–81). It found a place in Miller's celebrated *Gardeners Dictionary*, and of the many illustrations first prize for flamboyance goes to Weinmann in 1734 (Fig. 449). As in Cactaceae, so in Stapelieae it seems that the fattest, softest stems are the most prone to fasciate. *Larryleachia* (*Trichocaulon*) heads the list (Figs. 86, 454, 455). However, for out-of-this-world oddness I would give the prize to *Ceropegia stapeliiformis* (Fig. 452). *Orbea* (*Diplocyatha*) *ciliata* has already been mentioned (p. 33) for a phenomenon shared only with *Opuntia clavarioides*: dimorphic shoots, in which some regularly become ring-cristate and shaped like a mushroom with a depressed centre. Most if not all plants in cultivation seem to do this when well grown.

The only examples of variegation I have come across in the more or less succulent representatives of this Family is in *Hoya*, of which there are several cultivars, and *Ceropegia linearis* ssp. *woodii* which varies considerably when raised from seed, and a pale-margined variant is now generally available as 'Lady Heart' (Fig. 460).

Fig. 449 (Left) *Orbea variegata* 'Cristata' as featured in a Dutch picture-book of rare and exotic flowers in 1734. Compare with the real thing in Fig. 457. (GR)

Opposite page:

Fig. 450 (Upper right) Disorganized *Caralluma speciosa*, Somalia BS. (BJ)

Fig. 451 (Middle right) *Caralluma* sp. crest. (SR)

Fig. 452 (Lower right) *Ceropegia stapeliiformis* cristate bearing normal flowers. The typical species has long rubbery pendent or creeping stems 1 cm in diameter. (GR)

Asclepiadaceae

Fig. 453 (Left) *Duvalia pillansii* cristate. (HB)

Fig. 454 (Below) *Larryleachia marlothii* (*dinteri*) amazingly transmogrified in habitat. (GW)

Opposite page:

Fig. 455 (Above) *Larryleachia perlata,* also fasciated. (GW)

Fig. 456 (Below) *Orbea ciliata*: a ring cristation. (HM)

Asclepiadaceae

Asclepiadaceae

Opposite page:

Fig. 457 (Above) *Orbea variegata* crest. (HM)

Fig. 458 (Below) Madagascan *Stapelianthus pilosus* at Heidelberg University throwing up two crested branches. (GR)

Fig. 459 (Right) Twin crests on *Tavaresia barklyi* (*grandiflora*). Note that both branches apparently were triggered to fasciate simultaneously. (GR)

Fig. 460 (Below) *Ceropegia linearis* ssp. *woodii* 'Lady Heart', a Japanese cultivar name. (HM)

Apocynaceae, the Periwinkle Family

Fasciation is reported in 5 of the 14 species of the genus *Pachypodium* – all desirable "collector's pieces". A single record in the wild of *P. namaquanum* came first (Rowley 1999; Figs. 87-89, 461), and Mahr (1996) noted isolated reports for *P. succulentum* and *P. horombense*. *Pachypodium geayi* occasionally fasciates from seed; Fig. 462 was photographed in the U.S.A. in 1983 when it was considered a great rarity. That leaves the star of the show, *P. lamerei*, the most prolific in monster-production, thanks to mass propagation from seed each year to supply the demand for house plants. In addition to the thick-stemmed 'Curlycrest' (Fig. 464) there is a thin-stemmed version, rather like a green celosia (Fig. 465). I have had both from a single root, and wonder if we are faced with a chimera here with different layers of crest-forming cells (C) over a normal core (N) – perhaps CCN and CNN? Monstrose growth of *P. lamerei* has also been noted, including temporary production of broad obovate leaves (Figs. 466, 467) or outgrowths that suggest fat aerial roots but are not. Some crests are stable, others not; those that revert provide a useful source of cuttings to root up as grafting stock. Clearly we are facing a complicated genetical background here that awaits unravelling.

Apocynaceae

There are also at least two variegates of the same species. One is unremarkable, with occasional leaves splashed with paler green. The other, 'Particolour' (Figs. 468, 469) is much more striking with bright yellow patches randomly scattered. Both are seasonal, producing the most marked variegation in the spring and all-green leaves in the autumn. An unstable gene or genes are suspected, since repeated attempts at intergrafting with 4 other all-green species of *Pachypodium* have all failed to demonstrate a virus. A single plant of *P. namaquanum* with variegated foliage has been reported by Mahr (1996).

Adenium has finally obliged with a cristate - a large fan-like crest on *Adenium obesum* ssp. *socotranum* figured by Alain Christophe in his "Socotra, the lost island" p. 58, 2005. Collectors, eat your heart out! Variegations, however, are more within reach, thanks to intensive breeding. Hirose & Yokoi (1998) figure 'Snow Desert Brocade' with creamy white leaf margins, and another with streaking of the same colour, and cultivars with broad or narrow yellow margins are grown in India (Rowley 1999).

Opposite page:

Fig. 461 (Left) Solitary plant of *Pachypodium namaquanum* at Cauberg with the tip expanded into a 45 cm wide spathe-like crest. (GR)

Fig. 462 (Above right) *Pachypodium geayi*, one of the first cristate seedlings. (GR)

Fig. 463 (Below right) *Pachypodium lamerei* crest. (HM)

Fig. 464 (Above right) *Pachypodium lamerei* 'Curlycrest', the thick-stemmed cristate, which infrequently reverts. (GR)

Fig. 465 (Right) *Pachypodium lamerei*, the thin-stemmed cristate with reversions to normal shoots. (GR)

Fig. 466 (Above) *Pachypodium lamerei*, an anomalous shoot with broad leaves; highly reversible. (GR)

Fig. 467 (Below) Another *Pachypodium lamerei* variant. (FXS)

Opposite page:

Figs. 468, 469 (Above & Below) *Pachypodium lamerei* 'Particolour', the better of two variegations. (GR)

Apocynaceae

Asteraceae (Compositae), the Daisy Family

Examples of good, stable crests or variegates from the succulent quarters of the big Daisy Family are few and far between, but cherishable. Instances of fasciation in *Senecio* have been reported for *S. anteuphorbium* (Fig. 470), *S. articulatus*, *S. kleinia*, *S. radicans*, *S. serpens* 'Albert Baynes' (Fig. 475) and *S. stapeliiformis* ssp. *minor* 'Panoply' (Rowley 1994). Of these, the first four reverted or were not brought into cultivation. The last is a real beauty (Figs. 325, 476), and may be available by now in the U.S.A. *Senecio serpens* 'Albert Baynes' commemorates the Yorkshire zealot and co-founder of the National Cactus & Succulent Society in the U.K. It is worth preserving by rigorously weeding out any normal shoots that appear. *Othonna herrei* 'Cristata' as listed by Jacobsen was founded on a single crest found in the wild by Hans Herre but never brought into cultivation.

Many thick-stemmed senecios such as *S. articulatus*, *S. mweroensis* and *S. pendulus* are naturally variegated with purple arrowhead markings up the stem, one below each leaf base. However, there are three variegates that have arisen in cultivation and are worth hunting out. The over-familiar "candle plant", *Senecio articulatus*, is variable in joint size, shape and markings, but the clone 'Candlelight' (Fig. 471) has cream sectors on some of its leaves, is stable, as vigorous as the original and self-propagating. *S. rowleyanus* 'String of Pearls' (Fig. 474) arose in America and rivals the original in popularity; the amount of pallor on each leaf varies from 0% to 100%. *S. kleinia* 'Candystick' (Fig. 472) has already been discussed for its chance origin and subsequent refining from the dying stump of an old and unvariegated plant. This has recently gone one step further and produced crests (Fig. 473) that I am endeavouring to multiply as grafts on *S. ficoides*. A pale-margined cultivar of *S. jacobsenii* (*Kleinia petraea*) is reported from Japan (Hirose & Yokoi 1998: 155).

Asteraceae

Opposite page:

Fig. 470 (Above) *Senecio anteuphorbium*, a single fasciated branch from habitat that grew out normally. (GR)

Fig. 471 (Below) *Senecio articulatus* 'Candlelight', a good beginner's choice. (GR)

Fig. 472 (Above) *Senecio kleinia* 'Candystick', so named for the "vanilla and strawberry" look of the variegated foliage. (GR)

Fig. 473 (Below) *Senecio kleinia* 'Candystick' cristate, propagated as a graft on *S. ficoides*. (GR)

Fig. 474 (Top) The smallest pieces of *Senecio rowleyanus* 'String of Pearls' can be detached and rooted to start new colonies. (GR)

Fig. 475 (Above right) *Senecio serpens* 'Albert Baynes' responds to lush cultivation and removal of reversions. (HM)

Fig. 476 (Left) *Senecio stapeliiformis* ssp. *minor* 'Panoply', a sculptural gem if ever there was. (GR)

Crassulaceae, the Stonecrop Family

Crassulaceae are one of the three largest all-succulent Families, and their mostly fleshy stems and flattish leaves make for an imposing diversity of crests and variegates. Examples come from most of the genera, from tall shrubs down to the lowliest of rosettes and creepers. Add to this a general ease of propagation by offsets and cuttings, and it is no surprise to find many attractive novelties on offer by nurseries. Single leaves of many of them will grow, but you will be lucky if they do not all revert to normality. A minor reservation is that some of the best cultivars are unstable, and need to be kept in trim to avoid normal shoots overtaking the crest or variegated portion.

Beginning in Europe and with the hardiest representatives, we start with *Sedum* and the 'Cockscomb Stonecrop', a fasciation-prone variant of *S. rupestre* (*reflexum*) that has had a long history in gardens despite frequent reversions (Fig. 477, 522). Lloyd Praeger in his monographs of *Sedum* (1921) and the *Sempervivum* Group (1932) devotes a section to teratology making one wish that other monographers were equally considerate. For *Sedum* he has 4 cases of fasciation and 8 of variegation, not counting the purple-leaved variants of several species. He records 7 fasciated *Sempervivum* species (Fig. 478), 8 in *Aeonium* and 2 in *Monanthes*. Historically important is the fine painting in the Badminton Florilegium (Fig. 122) of *Aeonium arboreum* with two variegated sports, already cherished two centuries ago. Later along came 'Zwartkop', with dark purple, almost black foliage that is justly popular and common in gardens. In *Sedum* we have yellow- or white-edged foliage in *S. lineare* 'Variegatum', *S. kamtschaticum* 'Variegatum', *S. spurium* 'Tricolor' and an unnamed race of *S. makinoi*. In *S. sieboldii* 'Mediovariegatum' and *S. erythrostictum* (*alboroseum*) 'Variegatum' the pallor is in the centre of the leaf, and in *S. acre* we have clones with pale tips to the shoots at the start of the year ('Aureum' and 'Elegans').

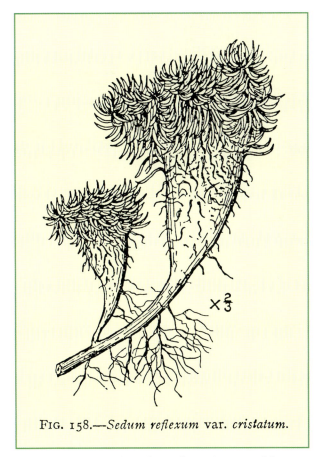

FIG. 158.—*Sedum reflexum* var. *cristatum*.

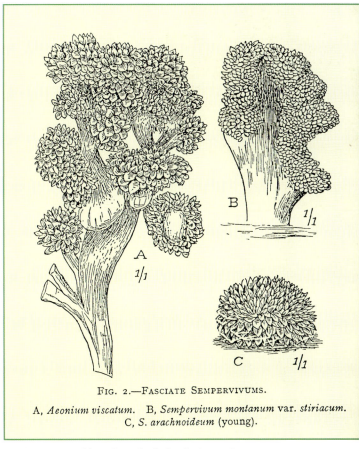

FIG. 2.—FASCIATE SEMPERVIVUMS.
A, *Aeonium viscatum*. B, *Sempervivum montanum* var. *stiriacum*.
C, *S. arachnoideum* (young).

Fig. 477 (Above left) *Sedum reflexum* 'Cristatum' from Praeger 1921, p. 271. Although perfectly hardy, it requires frequent trimming to remove reversions.

Fig. 478 (Above right) More fasciations from Praeger 1932: **A**. *Aeonium lindleyi* var. *viscatum*; **B**. *Sempervivum montanum* var. *stiriacum*; **C**. *Sempervivum arachnoideum*.

Crassulaceae

Opposite page:

Fig. 479 (Left) *Adromischus hemisphaericus* showing rare cristation of both the inflorescence and flowers. (DT)

Fig. 480 (Upper right) *Adromischus schuldtianus* variegated. (HM)

Fig. 481 (Middle right) *Aeonium simsii* crest. (BJ)

Fig. 482 (Lower right) *Aeonium tabuliforme* cristate tending to revert. An example in its prime is shown in Fig. 2. (GR)

Fig. 483 (Above) *Aeonium* 'Ballerina', an attractive vigorous and stable cv. with white upcurved leaf margins. (GR)

Fig. 484 (Right) *Aeonium arboreum* 'Variegatum'. (GR)

Fig. 485 (Above) *Aeonium* 'Harry Mak'. (GR)

Fig. 486 (Below) *Aeonium* 'Sunburst'. (HM)

Aichryson x *aizoides* 'Variegatum' is an old and trusted house plant (Praeger 1932) under the invalid name *A. domesticum* (Fig. 487). Some striking variegates of monocarpic *Orostachys iwarenge* have been bred in Japan (Kobayashi 2000 p.8; Fig. 514). They pose a propagation problem because the plant dies after flowering without branching. The nurseryman's way to propagate it is to scoop out the centre of a plant before the initiation of flowering to encourage it to produce offsets: once there is the least sign of the axis elongating it is too late. Tissue culture would seem to be the answer for mass propagation here. *O. spinosus* has produced some spectacular crests, as shown in 8 dramatic photographs by Richter (2003), and here in fig. 513.

Crassula hosts several striking variegates (Figs. 495-500) but surprisingly few cristates. *C. muscosa* (*lycopodioides* of old) 'Cristata' and 'Monstrosa' are among the few (Figs. 220, 329, 494). The new world Echeverioideae, with their rosettes of plump, colourful leaves, lend themselves to producing some sensational cristates, especially in *Echeveria* and its hybrids with *Pachyphytum*: x *Pachyveria* (Figs. 501-504).

Fig. 487 (Above) *Aichryson* x *aizoides* 'Variegatum', favoured in Victorian times as a windowsill plant. (GR)

Fig. 488 (Below) A striking mutant of the hardy *Chiastophyllum oppositifolium* variously known as 'Frosted Jade' and 'Jim's Pride'. (GR)

Fig. 489 (Above left) *Cotyledon orbiculata* variegated. (HM)

Fig. 490 (Above right) *Cotyledon tomentosa* 'White Palm', a choice variant with more cream colour than green in its foliage. (GR)

Fig. 491 (Left) *Cotyledon tomentosa* 'Yellow Palm', the reciprocal variegate. (HM)

Fig. 492 (Below) *Crassula conjuncta* variegated. (GR)

Opposite page:

Fig. 493 (Above) *Crassula* 'Gollum', a wonderful recent introduction with many synonyms, easy to grow and multiply from cuttings or leaves and not prone to revert to its progenitor *C. ovata*. (HM)

Fig. 494 (Below) *Crassula muscosa* monstrose. (HM)

Crassulaceae

Crassulaceae

Opposite page:

Fig. 495 (Top) *Crassula ovata* 'Obliqua Variegata'. (HM)

Fig. 496 (Centre) *Crassula ovata* variegated (small form). (HM)

Fig. 497 (Below left) *Crassula ovata* 'Hummel's Sunset'. (HM)

Fig. 498 (Below right) *Crassula rupestris* 'Whiteout'. (GR)

Fig. 499 (Above) *Crassula sarmentosa* 'Comet', an ideal beginners' plant but sprawling in habit and difficult to keep compact. (GR)

Fig. 500 (Right) The same; mutations to all yellow cannot survive independently, and reversions to all green are best cut out. (GR)

Crassulaceae

Opposite page:

Fig. 501 (Top left) *Echeveria agavoides* crest. (HM)

Fig. 502 (Top right) *Echeveria* hybrid 'Fantasia Carol'. (HM)

Fig. 503 (Middle left) *Echeveria glauca* var. *pumila* (*E. secunda*) crest. (HM)

Fig. 504 (Middle right) One of many cristate echeverias. This is an unnamed van Keppel hybrid: *E.* (*elegans* x *agavoides*) x *elegans*. (GR)

Fig. 505 (Bottom) *Echeveria pulvinata* 'Frosty' crest. (HM)

This page:

Fig. 506 (Top left) *Echeveria pulvinata* 'Tricolor', one of Harry Mak's naming. (HM)

Fig. 507 (Top right) *Echeveria purpusorum* variegated. (HM)

Fig. 508 (Right) *Kalanchoe blossfeldiana* 'Colour Spoon', one of many striking variants of this popular florists' flower. (GR)

Fig. 509 (Left) Another many-headed marvel, this time a cristate *Graptopetalum*. (HM)

Fig. 510 (Below left) *Kalanchoe manginii* 'Golden Nodding' from Harry Mak. (HM)

Fig. 511 (Bottom left) *Kalanchoe blossfeldiana* 'Variegata'. (HM)

Fig. 512 (Bottom right) *Kalanchoe fedtschenkoi* 'Painted Butterfly' showing progressive loss of chlorophyll towards the tip of the stem. (GR)

Opposite page:

Fig. 513 *Orostachys spinosus* crest, with a normal rosette at the front. (GR)

Crassulaceae

243

Fig. 514 (Top left) *Orostachys iwarenge* 'Fuji' from Japan, a short-lived beauty that is worth the effort of preserving it. (GR)

Fig. 515 (Middle left) *Orostachys* 'Phoenix'. (HM)

Fig. 516 (Bottom left) *Pachyphytum compactum* 'Brainwave'. (HM)

Opposite page:

Fig. 517 (Above) *Sedum album* 'Cristatum' outdoors. (HM)

Fig. 518 (Below) *Sedum erythrostictum* (*alboroseum*) variegated, outdoors. (HM)

Crassulaceae

Fig. 519 (Left) *Sedum lucidum* cristate. (GR)

Fig. 520 (Lower left) *S. pachyphyllum* 'Multifingers', one of many fine but tender crests from America. (GR)

Fig. 521 (Bottom) *Sedum* x *rubrotinctum* 'Aurora'. (HM)

Opposite page:

Fig. 522 (Above) *Sedum rupestre* 'Cristatum', a long survivor in gardens by regular pruning out of reversions. (GR)

Fig. 523 (Below) *Sedum sieboldii* 'Mediovariegatum', hardy but a martyr to slugs and snails; better in the cold frame or suspended. (GR)

Crassulaceae

Fig. 524 (Above) *Sempervivum* 'Botterbun', one of several occasional sports, all difficult to keep for long. (GR)

Fig. 525 (Below) *Sempervivum ciliosum* ssp. *octopodes* prodigiously fasciated. (GR)

Fig. 526 (Above) *Sempervivum* 'Fuzzy Wuzzy'. (HM)

Fig. 527 (Below) *Sempervivum grandiflorum* 'Hungry Puppy'. (HM)

Fig. 528 *Sinocrassula yunnanensis* cristate. (HB)

Agavaceae, the Century Plant family, and Dracaenaceae, the Dragon Tree Family

Taking Agavaceae in its original broad sense (including *Sansevieria*) we have here the finest and most diverse of all variegated leaf succulents. They are also the best researched, from the pioneer study on striped agaves by Trelease (1908) to the more recent investigations into *Sansevieria* by Chahinian (1986–1999). These have already been summarised in Chapters 2 and 3, so it remains only to figure further examples. *Sansevieria* variegates behave in the manner of three-layered chimeras; *Agave* seems to be two-layered only (Tilney-Bassett 1986). Hirose & Yokoi (1998: 31–33) figure 14 variegated agaves, some of them very striking, but only 2 sansevierias. For full coverage of that genus one must turn to the Chahinian publications, beginning with the admirable 1986 book covering variation within a single wild species, *S. trifasciata*. Here we figure just a few appetisers. Where plants produce offsets or suckers, however slowly, there is hope for the future. Solitary agaves can be made to offset by scooping out the growing tip, but it takes courage to risk destroying a unique show specimen to try. Some variants are more stable than others.

In *Agave americana* (Fig. 530), 'Striata' varies from leaf to leaf and from offset to offset; the other three plants in the picture are periclinal and rarely break up, but it can happen (see Fig. 287). Variegation is also found in several borderline succulents related to *Agave*: *Furcraea*, *Yucca*, *Dracaena*, *Cordyline*, *Nolina* and *Phormium*, many of these familiar in our gardens or as house plants. We are now deep in the realms of the monocots, so mention should also be made of the Family Bromeliaceae, which includes so many semi-succulent xerophytes favoured as indoor plants: *Billbergia*, *Cryptanthus*, *Tillandsia*, *Aechmea* and so on. Many of these are naturally variegated, but cultivars with additional striping are legion.

It would be tempting to declare that the stem anatomy of monocots, with its scattered vascular bundles rather than concentric cylinders of wood, in some way makes fasciation impossible, just as it rules out successful graft unions. Nature, however, delights in throwing up exceptions just as we think we have at last discovered an eternal truth. Out of all the thousands of happily stereotyped plants of *Agave shawii* growing in Baja California, just one left the crowd to grow the extravagantly fasciated inflorescence shown in Fig. 529. No Hollywood special effects department could match this for horrors: it was compared (in *Desert Plants* **7**: 114, 1985) to the pre-Columbian deity Xolotl who changed himself into a monstrose agave. Another crested agave with a fanlike apex is reported from Australia where a nurseryman sold it "for an astronomical price". Even more astonishing is the fan-topped *Dracaena draco* figured in Piante Grasse 19 (2) 1999: a sight to challenge the crested saguaros in symmetry and spectacle (Fig. 537).

Fig. 529 *Agave shawii* – an isolated inflorescence crest photographed in habitat by John Pasek in 1985.

Fig. 530 (Above) The four commonest variegates of *Agave americana*:- 'Mediopicta' (left), 'Mediopicta Alba' (centre, rear), 'Striata' (centre, front) and 'Marginata' (right). (GR)

Fig. 531 (Below) Another unusual variegated sport of *A. americana* in the Huntington Botanic Garden. (GR)

Fig. 532 (Above) *Agave filifera* crest. (HM)

Fig. 533 (Below) *Agave filifera* 'Afterglow' - one of the most sought after small agaves, but slow to offset. The new name replaces 'Compacta Variegata'. (GR)

Fig. 534 (Upper left) *Agave potatorum* 'Bonanza', a rare variegate. (SR)

Fig. 535 (Middle left) *Agave victoria-reginae*, 'Kazo Bana' (Flower of Kazo, according to Y. Hirose who named it), otherwise known as 'Golden Princess'. (GR)

Fig. 536 (Lower left) *Agave victoria-reginae* cristate, grown by Paul Hutchison of Tropic World. (PH)

Opposite page:

Fig. 537 (Above) *Dracaena draco* - a unique cristate reported to grow in habitat near Tenerife, and an Old World rival to the crested saguaros, figs. 5, 342. (FDS)

Fig. 538 (Below) An extravagantly fasciated rosette of a bromeliad, included here because of its rarity. (GR)

Agavaceae

255

Asphodelaceae, the Asphodel Family

Aloe arborescens is, according to Reynolds, the most widespread and commonly cultivated of all aloe species in South Africa, where it is used medicinally as an alternative to *A. vera*. A splendidly vigorous and flamboyantly striped cultivar of it is around under the name of 'Gold Rush', and does not suffer from reversions (Figs. 539, 540). Variegated aloes are not common, but they can be spectacular, as can be seen from 6 grown in Japan and illustrated by Hirose & Yokoi (1998: 36) (Fig. 541). They also figure 10 variegated haworthias and 3 gasterias. Leaf striping of varying intensity and colouring from white to yellow or pinkish adorns the leaves of these and adds welcome variety to an otherwise green-dominated field.

I have a single genuinely crested *Gasteria* (Fig. 554), and a large, vigorous specimen of *Bulbine latifolia* at Reading University regularly fans out at the tips of its inflorescences (Fig. 544). A fasciated *Haworthia arachnoidea* var. *setata* was illustrated in *Cactus Digest* **12**(4): 4, 2000 and correctly interpreted in *l.c.* **13**(1): 21, 2001 by Colin Walker. It subsequently reverted to a row of normal offsets, only one of which briefly went cristate again.

Asphodelaceae

Opposite page:

Figs. 539, 540 (Left and above right) *Aloe arborescens* 'Gold Rush', as vigorous and easy to multiply as the type. (GR, HM)

Fig. 541 (Below right) *Aloe ferox* 'Variegata'. (GR)

Fig. 542 (Above) *Aloe variegata* variegated. (HM)

Fig. 543 (Below) *Aloe* 'Green in Gold'. (HM)

Asphodelaceae

Opposite page:

Fig. 544 (Above left) Fasciated inflorescence of *Bulbine latifolia*. (GR)

Fig. 545 (Above right) Fasciated root of *Bulbine frutescens*. (GR)

Fig. 546 (Below) x *Gasteraloe* 'Green Ice'. (HM)

Fig. 547 (Top) *Gasteria bicolor* 'Golden Long Tongue'. (HM)

Fig. 548 (Middle) *Gasteria carinata* var. *verrucosa* variegated. (HM)

Fig. 549 (Bottom) *Gasteria disticha* (*obtusifolia*) 'Variegata'. (GR)

Asphodelaceae

Opposite page:

Figs. 550 (Top left) and 552 (Left centre) Two of many unnamed gasteria variegates. (HM & SR)

Fig. 551 (Top right) *Gasteria* 'Little Warty'. (HM)

Fig. 553 (Bottom) *Gasteria pillansii* variegate. (HM)

Fig. 554 (Above) *Gasteria* 'Royston's Fan', part cristate part monstrose. (HM)

Fig. 555 (Right) *Gasteria* sp.: a cristate inflorescence. (MP)

Harry Mak has built up an outstandingg collection of *Haworthia* cultivars in Manchester and has named at least 24 cultivars in his latest book (Mak 2003). He has generously lent photographs of some of his crests and variegates for inclusion here.

This page:

Fig. 556 (Top) *Haworthia attenuata* v. *radula* 'Golden Arrow'. (HM)

Fig. 557 (Middle) *Haworthia attenuata* 'White Arrow'. (HM)

Fig. 558 (Bottom) *Haworthia attenuata* 'Little Lemon'. (HM)

Opposite page:

Fig. 559 (Top left) *Haworthia attenuata* 'Sparkler'. (GR)

Fig. 560 (Top right) *Haworthia bolusii* crest. (HM)

Fig. 561 (Middle left) *Haworthia chloracantha* variegate. (HM)

Fig. 562 (Middle right) *Haworthia cooperi* v. *pilifera* 'Milky Cloud'. (HM)

Fig. 563 (Bottom left) *Haworthia cuspidata* variegate. (HM)

Fig. 564 (Bottom right) *Haworthia cymbiformis* 'Harry Mak' is perhaps the most widespread variegated *Haworthia*, and able to thrive with, apparently, surprisingly little chlorophyll. (GR)

Asphodelaceae

Asphodelaceae

Opposite page:

Fig. 565 (Top left) *Haworthia limifolia* 'Stripes'. (HM)

Fig. 566 (Top right) *Haworthia maxima* 'Dots-n-Streaks'. (HM)

Fig. 567 (Middle left) *Haworthia pygmaea* 'Fan of Woodstock'. (HM)

Fig. 568 (Middle right) *Haworthia pygmaea* hybrid variegate. (HM)

Fig. 569 (Bottom left) *Haworthia reinwardtii* hybrid variegate. (HM)

Fig. 570 (Bottom right) *Haworthia rigida* variegate. (HM)

This page:

Figs. 571, 572 (Top and middle right) *Haworthia subattenuata* 'Golden City'. (HM)

Fig. 573 (Bottom right) The same, as grown in full sun. (HM)

Fig. 574 (Upper left) *Haworthia truncata* variegate. (HM)

Fig. 575 (Upper right) *Haworthia truncata* var. *maughanii* variegate. (HM)

Fig. 576 (Middle left) *Haworthia turgida* variegate. (HM)

Fig. 577 (Middle right) *Haworthia viscosa* (*tortuosa*) variegate 'White Star'. (HM)

Fig. 578 (Bottom left) A variegated hybrid of *Haworthia viscosa*. (HM)

Aizoaceae, the Mesemb Family

This is the third of the three great all-succulent Families, and the least prone to teratology. Occasionally in large collections or nurseries one encounters twinned stems or forked or fused leaves, or stemless species with pale streaks or three leaves in a whorl in place of the usual two (Figs. 579, 584). These lapses rarely persist beyond the one season. The *National Cactus & Succulent Journal* **7**: 54, 1952 figures a *Pleiospilos* with what appears to be a cristate offset, but we have nothing further on how it subsequently developed. I had begun to fear that the Aizoaceae simply didn't know how to go cristate until I was shown the fine example of *Monilaria moniliformis* (Figs. 29, 580) from a collection quite near me in Reading (Rowley 2000).

What can be called "leaf cristation" has uniquely appeared in *Lithops*, as already revealed in Chapter 1 (Fig. 70). Another example in *L. aucampiae* with 9 lobes is figured in *Nat.Cact.Succ.J.* **36**: 116, 1981, and many-headed plants of *L. vallis-mariae* with 3-lobed and cristate growths in *Kakt. u. a. Sukk.* **52**: 96–97, 2001.

Aptenia is an untypical prostrate mesemb with flat, stalked leaves that is used for ground cover in frost-free countries. *A. cordifolia* 'Variegata' is a striking cultivar with the leaves marbled with pale yellow round the margins. A clone of *Glottiphyllum linguiforme* with streaks or flushes of yellow (Fig. 583) has been around for some time and was first pictured in *Nat.Cact.Succ.J.* **9**: 1954. Hirose & Yokoi (1998) figure variegated specimens of *Faucaria*, *Frithia* and *Pleiospilos*, and an anaemic *Conophytum*, but these may be the only examples of their kind. Variegation of a different sort occurs in a few *Lithops* species where the usual blend of purple-brown-yellow pigments is reduced or absent to give an overall greenish look – a colour rarely seen in the wild species. Named examples are *L. lesliei* 'Albinica', *L. fulviceps* 'Aurea' and *L. bromfieldii* 'Sulphurea'.

That most enigmatic of all *Lithops*, 'Steineckeana' (*L. steineckeana* Tisch.), qualifies for inclusion here as a true teratophyte. I am indebted to its biographer, Steven Hammer, for a summary of its extraordinary career (Hammer 2004). It arose as a chance seedling in cultivation, probably derived from *L. pseudotruncatella* pollinated by an unrelated species of *Argyroderma*, *Conophytum* or *Vanheerdea*. Certain seedlings show a cyclical behaviour, one year bearing the typical bilobed body with only vague markings, the next year having flatter tops with a large window and marbling more typical of *L. pseudotruncatella*. The following year the cycle begins anew. This cannot be a single chimerical clone because it occurs in several seedlings. Seed from "normal" 'Steineckeana' produces plants all true to the parental phenotype, or half normal and half cyclical. Clearly further testing is called for, especially from a cytologist.

Fig. 579 *Didymaotus lapidiformis* trilobed, photographed by Graham Williamson. (GW)

Fig. 580 (Above) *Monilaria moniliformis* cristate. (GR)

Fig. 581 (Below) *Faucaria* 'Star'. (HM)

Aizoaceae

Fig. 582 (Above) *Faucaria* 'Great Snow Stream' ex Japan. (HM)

Fig. 583 (Below) *Glottiphyllum linguiforme* 'Yellow Tongue'. (HM)

Fig. 584 (Above) *Lithops hookeri* var. *marginata* with three-lobed heads. (GR)

Fig. 585 (Below) *Oxalis peduncularis* fasciating, a lone representative of the Family Oxalidaceae. (SD)

Portulacaceae, the Purslane Family

Portulacaria afra, meritorious equally as a shrub for hedges in hot climates, as a bushy or bonsai houseplant and as an understock for grafting more delicate Portulacaceae, has to its further credit at least three variegates: 'Variegata' (alias 'Rainbow Bush', Fig. 587) and 'Tricolor' with yellow leaf edges, and an apparently unnamed cultivar with yellow centres to the leaves. In my experience the variegates are more delicate than the type and prone to sunburn. *Portulaca* 'Coral Ice' has yellow-margined leaves, as does a variant of *Talinum crassifolium,* and Hirose & Yokoi (1998) also illustrate a particoloured *Lewisia cotyledon.* In *Anacampseros* we have one welcome colour variation in *A. rufescens* 'Sunrise' (Fig. 586) with yellow to pink tips to the leaves.

Fig. 586 (Right) *Anacampseros rufescens* 'Sunrise', the only variegate so far reported for this genus. (GR)

Fig. 587 (Below) *Portulacaria afra* 'Rainbow Bush'. (GR)

Passifloraceae, the Passionflower Family

A single genus, *Adenia*, represents this Family in succulent plant collections, with some bizarre pachycaul climbers and caudiciforms. Although favoured by only a minority of specialist growers, no genus however obscure seems to be immune to occasional genetical lapses. In response to my pleas to friends to look out for these, Len Newton came up with two worthy instances for *Adenia*, shown here from his slides as figs. 588 and 589.

Fig. 588 (Left) Cristate branch of *Adenia globosa* ssp. *pseudoglobosa* found in the wild and rooted as a cutting. However, as so often happens with hard-wooded crests, all the sideshoots produced were normal. (LN)

Fig. 589 (Below) *Adenia globosa* ssp. *globosa*, one of many fasciated branches that appeared on a cultivated plant in Nairobi. (LN)

Didiereaceae, the Old World Cactus Family

With 4 genera and just 11 species, these rare Madagascan endemics have not yet had a chance to diversify in cultivation, but the rising interest in them has brought to light the first cristate (Fig. 590), and it could not have arrived at a better place (Werner Rauh's collection in Heidelberg) to ensure its preservation and, if possible, distribution.

Fig. 590 (Right) *Alluaudia procera* - the first fasciation found in Didiereaceae, discovered, photographed & propagated by Werner Rauh. (WR)

Fig. 591 (Below) Another crest from the same plant. (WR)

Epilogue
chapter 11

This book came about in part from the urge to remove prejudice and fill a gap in the literature; in part from vexation that so little serious study is devoted to these wonders of nature. What basic research has been done is largely on non-succulent plants, and we are left to make our own guesses by analogy when trying to understand aberrant succulents. Many of the unsolved problems lie within the reach of amateur experimenters: raising suspected chimeras from root cuttings, testing for virus by grafting, attempting to create chimeras and raising seed to see what is inherited and what is not. I hope that this first modern attempt to survey the field may inspire readers to pick up the gauntlet. Don't just collect plants like stamps in an album: ask questions and take steps to pry out the answers.

It has been said that teratophytes of the type considered here have no place in nature; that they are ill-adapted and could not survive long. That is not entirely true at present, nor need it remain so in the future. Variegation of a sort we have seen to exist in many wild species, from *Sansevieria* to *Maranta*, from bromeliads to *Solenostemon* (*Coleus*). Fasciation has never become the norm in any wild plant, although there are situations in which it could bring advantages, as in the leaflike expansion of the side branches of *Euphorbia woodii* 'Salad Bowl' (Fig. 51) into cladodes better adapted for life in a shady glasshouse. There is indeed one niche in nature where flat, convoluted, ribbonlike stems benefit the plant: the tropical lianas (Kerner & Oliver 1: 475-477, 734 (1894)). Examples are *Bauhinia* and *Rhynchosia*, both in the Leguminosae (Fig. 592). These wind themselves tightly round supporting tree trunks, but have to be able to stretch as the trunk expands. The undulations and con-

Fig. 592 Flat ribbon-like stems of lianas: NOT fasciated (Kerner & Oliver 1894).

tortions of the flat stems allow for this. But although they look so much like fasciations, they are not: they have a normal meristem and flatness is achieved by anomalous secondary thickening in one plane only.

Ability to fasciate or variegate lies dormant within the make-up of most if not all higher plants, a tiny element within their DNA among the countless numbers of codings that have accumulated in the course of their evolution from simpler beginnings. With a flight of imagination, consider what might happen if fasciations happened to have better survival against radiation, or if variegation somehow protected a plant from global warming. One-in-a-billion heritable types could be favoured, and what we now call a freak or *lusus naturae* could become the norm, just as we accept aerial roots, stipules and bulbs as the norm for certain types of plants. The teratophobes would finally be confounded – if there were any left to confound.

It would have been satisfying to end by dispelling the mysteries and mythology surrounding teratophytes and assert that science has come up with an answer for everything. That this is not so is due more to a lack of trying than to a lack of means. If these plants were rated as important as food crops, modern technology would have been called in to unravel their secrets long ago. Then, shorn of magic and bereft of hidden depths they would stand bare and unloved, for who can enthuse over something where there is nothing left to discover? Fortunately, that situation is unlikely in the near future. The banter can go on over why leaves go striped or why the most expensive cristates are always the first to revert. And the mysteries are not confined to the plants, either. Why do some people hate them as sick and ugly, while others pay high prices for a green tumescent blob or tiny splash of yellow? To me, cristates extend the range of sculptural shapes in a collection, just as variegates break the monotony of all-green stems and leaves. Chimeras justify their existence by the surprise element, as well as by serving science in showing how different layers of tissue contribute to growth and morphology.

I have just enjoyed eating a navel orange: as sure an example of teratology as any, with one malformed baby orange stillborn inside another. Yet we accept it without a murmur because of the delicious flavour and the sterility that removes the pips. So to teratophobes the world over I can only admonish: "It's all in the mind, you know!".

Now, what's on the television tonight? Oh, "The Monster that challenged the World". But who loves monsters, anyway? Teratopia, here I come …

Fig. 593 *Euphorbia woodii* 'Bighead Medusa'. (GR)

Fig. 594 (Left) *Opuntia ficus-indica* 'Reticulata', a curious mutant that nevertheless flourishes in cultivation (GR), and something similar (Fig. 595, above), perhaps the same clone?, as figured by Dillenius in 1732.

Glossary

The following definitions cover only the less familiar terms, or those new or used in a sense special to teratophytes. Normal botanical terms such as petal and petiole will be found in the glossary of my "Name that Succulent" (1980); the best independent volume is Urs Eggli's "Glossary of botanical terms with special reference to Succulent Plants" (1993).

Anthocyanin – One of the basic water-soluble glycoside pigments responsible for red, purple and blue colours in plants.
Auxin – Plant growth substance that stimulates elongation of shoots and roots. *Cf.* Cytokinin.
Betalain – One of the water-soluble nitrogenous pigments contributing beetroot-red colouring (betacyanins) or yellow (betaxanthins).
Carotenoid – One of the yellow, orange or red fat-soluble pigments, typical of carrots.
Chim[a]era – In botany, a plant composed of a mixture of two or more genetically different tissues.
Chloroplast – Lens-shaped body containing chlorophyll, the green pigment that activates photosynthesis.
Chlorosis – Yellowing caused by loss of green chlorophyll.
Chromoplast – Any coloured plastid: green from chlorophyll, orange from carotin, etc.
Crest (Adj. **Crested**) – Plant or part of a plant showing fasciation.
Cristate (Noun or adj.) – See **Crest**.
Cytokinin – Plant growth substance that stimulates cell division. *Cf.* Auxin.
Dichotomy – Forking; division into two equal branches.
Endogenous – Of deep-seated origin. *Cf.* Exogenous (Fig. 296).
Exogenous – Of superficial origin. *Cf.* Endogenous.
Fasciation – Growth abnormality in which a point meristem broadens into a fan. *Cf.* Crest.
Flavone – One of a group of pigments associated with the yellow colour of primroses.
I.C.B.N. – International Code of Botanical Nomenclature.
I.C.N.C.P. – International Code of Nomenclature for Cultivated Plants.
Mericlinal – Comprising an arc. *Cf.* Periclinal, Sectorial.
Meristem – The mass of undifferentiated cells forming the growing tip of any organ.
Monstrose – Having disorganised growth with a loss of symmetry.
Monstrosity – Any type of abnormality resulting from disorganised growth; a plant thus affected.
Multiplex – As applied to crests, having many meristems packed closely side by side. *Cf.* Phalangial.
Mutagen – An agent that increases the rate of mutation.
Mycoplasma – An infective body combining features of bacteria and viruses but lacking a firm cell wall.
Ontogeny – Expansion of an organism from birth to death.
Periclinal – Parallel to the surface. *Cf.* Mericlinal, Sectorial.
Phalangial – As applied to crests, having a single linear meristem. *Cf.* Multiplex.
Plastid – A structure enclosed within a membrane that carries out a function in the cytoplasm, as for instance the lens-shaped chloroplast.
Proliferation – In teratology, abnormally free growth resulting in excessive branching or expansion of normally dormant apices.
Reciprocal Variegation – Occurrence of a pair of variegates showing an interchange of green and non-green areas, brought about by reversal of the appropriate tissue layers (See p. 76).
Sectorial – Comprising a sector formed by two radii of a circle. *Cf.* Mericlinal, Periclinal.
Teratology – The study of all abnormal types of growth. Greek: *teratos*, a monster.
Teratophile – A lover of teratophytes.
Teratophobe – A hater of teratophytes.
Teratophyte – A plant with abnormal growth.
Variegation – Bi- or multi-coloured effect resulting from a localised failure of pigment to develop.
Vascular system – The continuous network of conducting tissue of a plant.

Appendix 1

Recommended Plants

BEGINNER'S CHOICE

Available, easy to maintain, fast growing on own roots.

a. *Cristates*

CACTACEAE
Opuntia imbricata 'Cristata'
Echinopsis spachiana 'Cristata'
Mammillaria elongata 'Cristata'
Mammillaria bocasana 'Multilanata Cristata'

EUPHORBIACEAE
Euphorbia lactea 'Cristata'

CRASSULACEAE
Echeveria setosa 'Candy Floss' and choice of several other species and hybrids.
Sedum rupestre 'Cristatum'

b. *Variegates*

AGAVACEAE
Agave americana 'Marginata'
Sansevieria trifasciata 'Laurentii'

CRASSULACEAE
Aeonium 'Ballerina'
Aichryson x *aizoides* 'Variegatum'
Crassula sarmentosa 'Comet'
C. rupestris 'Whiteout'
Kalanchoe blossfeldiana (edge-striped)
Sedum sieboldii 'Mediovariegatum'

ASPHODELACEAE
Aloe arborescens 'Gold Rush'

EUPHORBIACEAE
Euphorbia abyssinica 'Milky Totem'
E. submammillaris 'Indian Corn'

ASTERACEAE
Senecio rowleyanus 'String of Pearls'

Appendix

c. *Monsters*

CACTACEAE
Cereus 'Abnormis' ('Peruvianus Monstrosus')
Echinopsis lageniformis 'Jock, Dick & Willy'
Echinopsis chamaecereus 'Crassicaulis Cristata'
Mammillaria 'Fred', 'Freaky' and choice of several others
Opuntia 'Maverick'

CONNOISSEUR'S CHOICE

Harder or more expensive to get; need more care
[**G**] = best grafted

CACTACEAE
Pachycereus schottii 'Monstrosus' & 'Mieckleyanus'
Carnegiea gigantea (cristate)
   + many scarce or "one-off" crests or variegates of favourite dwarf genera:
   Ariocarpus, Astrophytum, Gymnocalycium, Mammillaria, etc. [Some **G**]
   + *Hylogymnocalycium* 'Singular' (Chimera) [**G**]

EUPHORBIACEAE
Euphorbia obesa 'Rocky Mountain' [**G**]
Euphorbia piscidermis 'Cristata' [**G**]

APOCYNACEAE
Pachypodium lamerei 'Curlycrest' (cristate)
Pachypodium lamerei 'Particolor' (variegated)

ASCLEPIADACEAE
Larryleachia (*Trichocaulon*), *Tavaresia* and other occasional crests. [**G**]
Orbea ciliata (ring cristate)

AGAVACEAE
Agave: variegates of smaller-growing species, e.g. *A. filifera* 'Afterglow', *A. victoria-reginae*
   'Kazo Bana' (edge - striped)
Sansevieria: variegates of species other than *S. trifasciata*.

CRASSULACEAE
Orostachys iwarenge 'Fuji'

Appendix 2

Innovations

Building a collection of succulent cultivars is not made any easier by the lack of names for many of the choicer clones. Worse, many commonly used names, including latinised *cristatus* and *variegatus*, are outlawed by the draconian Codes and have to be replaced.

Outside of Japan, only one recent writer, Harry Mak, has taken cultivars seriously and formally published several names (Mak 2003).

To his listing the following are added here:

	Page
1. Cristate variants of normal species	
Euphorbia suzannae 'Maelstrom' (cristate + variegated)	204
Euphorbia woodii 'Salad Bowl'	29
Pachyphytum compactum 'Brainwave'	244
Senecio stapeliiformis 'Panoply'	167, 230
2. Plants variegated in leaves, stems or both	
Aeonium 'Harry Mak'	86, 234
Agave filifera 'Afterglow'	253
Agave potatorum 'Bonanza'	254
x *Alworthia* 'Fantasy'	142-143
Crassula rupestris 'Whiteout'	238
Haworthia cymbiformis 'Harry Mak'	23, 263
3. Monstrose variants	
Cleistocactus strausii 'Quantum Leap' (mostrose + cristate)	129
Echinopsis lageniformis 'Jock, Dick & Willy'	109
Mammillaria 'Freaky'	105, 279
Rebutia (*krainziana*) 'Haywire'	132
Rebutia (*krainziana*) 'Prodigy'	121
x *Sclerinocereus* 'John White' (*Sclerocactus* x *Echinocereus*)	105, 124
4. Proliferations	
Opuntia ficus-indica 'Eyeful' (proliferous and variegated)	121, 136
Opuntia 'Maverick'	112, 279
5. Spiral torsion	
Cereus 'Vortex'	116, 140
6. Chimeras	
+ *Uebelechinopsis* 'Treetopper' (*Echinopsis* + *Uebelmannia*)	100-101

These are all relatively stable, distinctive, durable and propagatable, as distinct from a majority of cultigens for which a pet name would serve no useful purpose. Standard specimens have not been prepared, but the accompanying illustrations here should establish the identity of each cultigen better than preserved material.

Bibliography
chapter 14

BACKEBERG, C. (1934): A new, large-flowered cristate. *Cactus J.(G.B.)* **2**: 73.
    [*Lobivia silvestrii* 'Crassicaulis cristata'. See also *Blätter f.Kakt.* **l**(8): Cristata 2, 1934.]
BAUSOR, S.C. (1937): Fasciation and its relation to problems of growth. *Bull.Torrey Bot.Club* **64**: 383–400, 445–475.
BOKE, N.H. (1951): Histogenesis of the vegetative shoot in *Echinocereus*. *Amer.J.Bot.* **38**: 23–38.
BOKE, N.H. (1976): Dichotomous branching in *Mammillaria* (Cactaceae). *Amer.J.Bot.* **63**: 1380–1384.
BOKE, N.H. & ROSS, R.G. (1978): Fasciation and dichotomous branching in *Echinocereus* (Cactaceae). *Amer.J.Bot.* **65**(5): 522–530.
BORG, J. (1937): *Cacti.* Cristate forms and other monstrosities pp.40–42.
    [Advice on creating them artificially to be taken with a large pinch of salt!]
BRADLEY, R. (1718): *New improvements of planting and gardening.* **I**. 72pp., Mears, UK.
    [Graft-transmissable variegation p.6.]
BRANDHAM, P. (1974): A double *Gasteria*. *Nat.Cact.Succ.J.* **29**: 81–82.
BURBIDGE, F.W. (1877): *Cultivated plants–their propagation and improvement.* 620pp., Blackwood & Son, UK.
BURRAS, J.K. (1997): Streaks and Sectors. *The Garden* **122**: 12–15.
BYLES, R.S. (1957): *Sempervivum tectorum* v. *calcareum* cv. nov. 'Grigg's Surprise' *Nat.Cact.Succ.J.* **12**: 70–72.
CARRIÈRE, E.A. (1865): *Production et Fixation des Variétés dans les Végétaux.* 72 pp., Paris.
    [Amateurish compilation, completely without references. P.50 *Opuntia cylindrica cristata*.]
CHAHINIAN, B.J. (1986): *The Sansevieria trifasciata varieties.* 109pp., Trans Terra, USA.
CHAHINIAN, B.J. (1992–94): The Variegated Corner. *Sansevieria J.* **l**: 14–16, 29–31, 53–56, 75–77, 1992; **2**: 21–24, 46–48, 70–72, 92–93, 1993; **3**: 22–23, 46–48, 1994.
CHAHINIAN, B.J. (1993): Variegation in cultivated sansevierias. *Haseltonia* **1**: 45–54.
CHAHINIAN, B.J. (1999): Variegated sansevierias. *Cactus & Co.* **3**: 43–47, 66–69.
CHURCH, A.H. (1904): *On the relation of phyllotaxis to mechanical laws.* 353pp. London, UK.
DAWSON, E.Y. & RUSH, H.G. (1954): A monstrose *Selenicereus* from Cuba. *Cact.Succ.J.(U.S.)* **26**: 180–181.
DRAWERT, J. (1983): Chimärenbildung bei *Eriocereus jusbertii* (Rebut) Riccobono. *Kakt.u.a.Sukk.* **34**: 2–4.
DUBROVSKY, J.G. (2002): Tumorous malformations in natural populations of *Pachycereus* and its associated mistletoe. *Cact.Suc.Mex.* **47**: 46, 48-56, 70-71.
GATES, H.E. (1930): Cristates. *Cact.Succ.J.(U.S.)* **2**: 273–274.
GENTRY, H.S. (1982): *Agaves of Continental North America.* 670pp., Univ. Arizona Press, USA.
GRAHAM, D. (1962): In quest of crests. *Cact.Succ.J.(U.S.)* **34**: 156–159.
GRÄSER, R. (1960): Ueber *Opuntia tuna monstrosa*. *Kakt.u.a.Sukk.* **11**: 33–35.
HAMMER, S. (2004): The Adventure of the Second Stein. *Mesemb Study Group Bull.* **19**: 55-56.
HESTER, J.P. (1940): *Carnegiea gigantea cristata* or crested sahuaros. *Desert Plant Life* **12**: 84–87, 109–111. [Good survey of stages in crest formation, with 17 photographs, but Lamarckian interpretation!]
HIROSE, Y. (2000): Crossing haworthias–the dream of developing new *Haworthia* cultivars. *Haworthiad* **14**: 30–33.
HIROSE, Y. & YOKOI, M. (1998): *Variegated Plants in Color.* 296pp., Japan.
    [Over 1400 col. plates.]
HORWOOD, F.K. (1983): Some notes on the grafting of euphorbias. *Euphorbia J.* **1**: 29–30.
HOUGHTON, A.D. (1930): *The Cactus Book.* 147pp. Macmillan, USA. [Chapter X–Cristates, Variegates and Monstrose forms, pp.57–64.]
HUNTER, M. (1987): Bizarre beauties. *Garden (U.S.)* **11**(3): 6–9 and covers.
    [Fasciated plants, including 3 colour plates of saguaros.]
HUNTER, M. (1988): Collecting crested & monstrose euphorbias. *Euph.J.* **5**: 21–25.

JEFFRIES, L. & SMALE, T. (1971): Are fasciated growths in cacti caused by microbial infections? *Cact.Succ.J.(G.B.)* **33**: 92–93.

JONES, W.N. (1934): *Plant Chimaeras and Graft Hybrids*. 136pp., Methuen.

JONSSON, G. (1969): Recherches ontogéniques sur une anomalie spontanée du *Stapelia* … . *Rev.Gen.Bot.* **76**: 37–74. [Fasciation in *Orbea*.]

JONSSON, G. & GORENFLOT, R. (1970): Etude comparée de divers aspects structuraux de la fasciation… *Bull.Soc.Bot.France, Mem.* 1970, **117**: 113–142. [*Stapelia, Armeria* & *Plantago*.]

KEPPEL, J.C.V. (1971): *Echeveria* 'Hoveyi' and *Echeveria* 'Zahnii'. *Nat.Cact.Succ.J.* **26**: 101–102.

KERNER, A. & OLIVER, F.W. (1894–1895): *The Natural History of Plants*. 2 Vols. Blackie & Son, UK.

KNOX, A.A. (1908): The Induction, Development and Heritability of Fasciations. *Carnegie Inst.Washington Pubn.* **98**. 21pp., USA. [Confined to experiments on *Oenothera*.]

KOBAYASHI, A. (2000): Cacti & succulents in Japan: Part 4: Chimeras and others. *Cact.Succ.J.(U.S.)* **72**: 4–13, 71-79.

LEAL, A.R. (1946): Teratologia en *Pterocactus*…. *Lilloa* **12**: 61–66. [7 plates. Extravagantly fasciated stems and flowers of *Pterocactus* from a normal tuber.]

LINDSAY, G. (1962): Giant Crests. *Cact.Succ.J.(U.S.)* **34**: 172–174.

LINDSAY, G. (1963): The Genus *Lophocereus*. *Cact.Succ.J.(U.S.)* **35**: 176–192.

MAHR, D. (1996): *Pachypodium* Oddities. *Cact.Succ.J.(U.S.)* **68**: 200–204.

MAK, H. (1993-2003): *Photo Album of Succulents in Color*. Vols. 1-3. In English and Chinese.

MASTERS, M.T. (1869): *Vegetable Teratology*. Ray Society, UK.

MIKHALTSOV, A. (2000): [Russian with English summary] *Cactus Club* 2000 (5): 4–11. [Cactus variegates].

MILLER, P. (1731): *The Gardeners Dictionary*. 833pp., Miller, UK. [First Edition in folio.]

MOQUIN-TANDON, A. (1841): *Elements de Teratologie Vegetale*. Paris, France.

PENZIG, O. (1890–94): *Pflanzen Teratologie*. 3 Vols. Germany. [Edn.II in 1921. Bibliography of 283 pages. See note in Wolthuys 1948 p.25.]

PUSEY, J.G. (1962): *Sedum* 'Aurora'–a possible chimaera. *Nat.Cact.Succ.J.* **17**:11–12, 31.

RAUH, W. (1988): Unusual growth in succulent euphorbias–fasciation & dichotomous branching. *Euph.J.* **5**: 7–17.

RICHTER, I. (2003): Cristate *Orostachys* pictures. *Avonia* **21**: 14-15.

ROST, E.C. (1932): *Cereus caesius monstrosus*. *Desert*, Cactus number, May 1932: 1, 6–7. [Proof of inherited monstrosity.]

ROWLEY, G.D. (1947): Pitcher formation in *Bryophyllum daigremontianum* Bgr. *Nat.Cact.Succ.J.* **2**: 79.

ROWLEY, G.D. (1954): Plants in 3D … a note on fasciation in succulents. *Nat.Cact.Succ.J.* **9**: 61–63.

ROWLEY G.D. (1980): What is 'Haku-Jo'? *Nat.Cact.Succ.J.* **35**: 22.

ROWLEY, G.D. (1984): Ring Cristates–a rare type of fasciation. In LAMB, B. & S. *The Monthly Notes on the Exotic Collection*. Feb. 1984: 11, 13–15.

ROWLEY, G.D. (1985a): A cristate *Lithops*. In LAMB, B. & S. *The Monthly Notes on the Exotic Collection*. April 1985: 32–33, 34.

ROWLEY, G.D. (1985b): Spiral Torsion in Succulents. *Brit.Cact.Succ.J.* **3**: 58–60.

ROWLEY, G.D. (1989): + *Hylocalycium*, the first bigeneric cactus chimaera. *Cact.Succ.J.(U.S.)* **61**: 168–170.

ROWLEY, G.D. (1993): Unexpurgated adventures of a Ring-cristate *Lobivia*. *Brit.Cact.Succ.J.* **11**: 10–11.

ROWLEY, G.D. (1994): *Succulent Compositae*. 238pp., Strawberry Press, USA.

ROWLEY, G.D. (1997a): *A History of Succulent Plants*. 409pp., Strawberry Press, USA.

ROWLEY, G.D. (1997b): Two cacti in one: +*Hylocalycium*. *Cactus File* **2**(12): 8.

ROWLEY, G.D. (1997c): Cristate succulents–a naming dilemma. *Brit.Cact.Succ.J.* **15**: 202–203.

ROWLEY, G.D. (1999): *Pachypodium* and *Adenium, Cactus File Handbook* **5.**

ROWLEY, G.D. (2000): *Monilaria moniliformis*–a rare cristate plant. *Mesemb Study Group Bull.* **15**: 12–13.

ROWLEY, G.D. (2003): Cristates, variegates and the asymmetric universe. *Brit.Cact.Succ.J.* **21**: 41-44.

ROWLEY, G.D. (2005): + *Hylogymnocalycium* replaces + *Hylocalycium* (cactus chimera). *Brit. Cact. Succ. J.* **23**: 12.

RUSSELL, J. (1939): Cacti–hybrid, grafted and monstrous. *Cactus Journal (G.B.)* **8**: 1–5. ["They fiddle with the works of God and make them seem uncommon odd."]

Bibliography

SATO, T. (1998): *Nishiki Cactus Handbook*. 64pp. Japan Cactus Planning Co., Japan.
SATO, T. (1999): *Cristata Cactus Handbook*. 64pp. Japan Cactus Planning Co., Japan.
SATO, T. (1999): *Nishiki Succulent Handbook*. 64pp. Japan Cactus Planning Co., Japan.
 [Eye-dazzling collections of colour plates of variegations and cristations, 600 in each book.]
SHURLY, E. (1959): *Cacti*. 160pp., Ward Lock & Co., UK.
 [Chapter 9: Cristates, pp.83–87, with 2 page list of cristate cacti.]
SNYDER, E.E. & WEBER, D.J. (1966): Causative factors of cristation in the Cactaceae. *Cact.Succ.J.(U.S.)* **38**: 27–32.
SOMBRERO, C. (1966): Enigma of Variegations. *New Plantsman* **3**(3): 158–169.
SUGURI, K. & SATO, T. (1996): *Ariocarpus Hand Book Cultivated in Japan*. 72pp., Japan Cactus Planning Co., Japan. [357 colour plates. In Japanese.]
TILNEY-BASSETT, R.A.E. (1986): *Plant Chimaeras*. 199pp., E. Arnold, UK.
TRELEASE, W. (1908): *Variegation in the Agaveae*. 27pp., Wiesner-Festschrift, Germany. [7 plates.]
UITEWAAL, A.J.A. (1959): *Epiphyllum* f. *cristata* [sic!]. *Succulenta* 1959: 12-13.
WEISS, F.E. (1933): Variegated foliage. *Proc.Linn.Soc.London* **145**(3): 135–149.
WHITE, A. & SLOANE, B.L. (1937): *The Stapelieae*. 3 Vols. Abbey San Encino Press, USA.
WHITE, O.E. (1948): Fasciation. *Bot.Rev.* **14**(6): 319–358.
WOLTHUYS, J.J.V. (1938): *The Enigma of the Origin of Monstrosity and Cristation in Succulent Plants*. Edn.I. 73pp., De Torenlaan, Netherlands.
WOLTHUYS, J.J.V. (1948): *The Enigma of the Origin of Monstrosity and Cristation in Succulent Plants*. Edn.II. 111pp., De Torenlaan, Netherlands.
 [In English & Dutch.]
WORSDELL, W.C. (1905): Fasciation–its meaning and origin. *New Phyt.* **4**: 55–74.
WORSDELL, W.C. (1915–16): *The principles of Plant Teratology*. 2 Vols. Ray Society, UK.
 [Marred by archaic, teleological attempts at interpretation.]

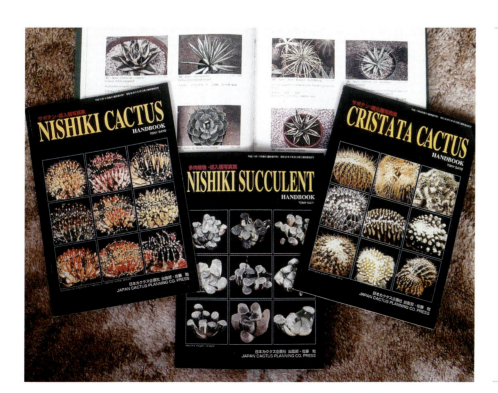

Fig. 596
Some literature from Japan on succulent teratophytes, which have long been propagated and cherished there. (GR)

Index

Numbers in **bold type** denote illustrations, with or without accompanying text

Abutilon 74
Acanthocalycium spiniflorum **12**
    violaceum **12**
Acanthocereus tetragonus **117**
Adenia 272
    globosa **272**
Adenium 147
    obesum 225
        'Snow Desert Brocade' 225
Adromischus cristatus 140
    hemisphaericus **232**
    schuldtianus **232**
Aechmea 251
Aeonium 231
    arboreum **63**, 231
        'Crested Sunburst' 134
        'Variegatum' **63**, **233**
        'Zwartkop' **144**
    'Ballerina' 146, **233**, 278
    'Harry Mak' **86**, **234**
    lindleyi **231**
    simsii **232**
    'Spreading Sun' **20**
    'Sunburst' **87**, 82 **137**, **234**
    tabuliforme **7**, **232**
Agavaceae 251-255
Agave 38, 146, 172, 279
    americana **77**, 81, **142**, **252**
        'Marginata' ....
        ...7, **77**, 81, **82**, 142, **252**, 278
        'Marginata Alba' **82**
        'Marginata Pallida' 82
        'Mediopicta' **77**, 82, **252**
        'Mediopicta Alba' ..**77**, **82**, **252**
        'Striata' ..**77**, **82**, 93, 251, **252**
    filifera **253**
               'Afterglow'   **253**, 279
    fourcroydes 80
    potatorum 'Bonanza' **85**, **254**
    shawii 251
    variegation patterns 75, 76, **77**
    victoria-reginae **254**
        'Golden Princess' **254**
        'Kazo Bana' **254**, 279
Agrobacterium tumefaciens 110
Aichryson aizoides **235**, 278
    domesticum 235
Aizoaceae 172, 267-270
Albinism 63
Alluaudia procera 147, **273**
Aloe **36**, 38, 172
    arborescens 256
        'Gold Rush' **256**, 278
    bellatula 142
    descoingsii **74**
    ferox **256**
    'Green in Gold' **257**
    maculata 74
    saponaria 74
    variegata 74, **257**
    vera 256
    x *Alworthia* 'Fantasy' 142, **143**
Anacampseros rufescens **271**
Anthocyanin 64
Apocynaceae 224-227
Aporocactus See *Disocactus*
x *Aporoheliocereus* See *Disocactus*

Aptenia 267
    cordifolia 267
Araucaria 38, 138
Ariocarpus 50, 125, 172, 279
    agavoides x *kotschoubeyanus* ....
    ....**70-72**
    fissuratus 133
    hybrids **70-73**
    kotschoubeyanus ....
    ....**96**, **97**, 133, **173**
    retusus **52**, **174**, **175**, **201**
    retusus x *scaphirostris* **73**
    scaphirostris **96**
    trigonus See *retusus*
Asclepiadaceae 218-223
Asphodelaceae 256-266
Asteraceae 228-230
Astrophytum
    ....125, **128**, 172, **179**, **200**, 279
    asterias **89**, 133
    asterias x *myriostigma* **88**
    chimerical hybrid 103, **104**
    myriostigma ....
    ....**129**, **175**, **176**, **200**
    'Onzuka' **105**
Aztekium 116, 172
    ritteri 133, **166**

Bailey, Geoff 70
    collection **70-73**
Barad, Jerry 109
Bauhinia 274
Baynes, Albert 228
Beaufort, Duchess of 63
Bergerocactus emoryi 46, **48**
Betalain 64
Bifacial fasciation **25**
Bilateral fasciation **25**
Billbergia 251
Blossfeldia liliputana **176**
Bowiea 38
Bradley, Richard 63, 74
Bromeliaceae, bromeliads
    ....74, 251, **255**, 274
Bulbine frutescens **258**
    latifolia 256, **258**

Cactaceae ....172 *et seq.*
Cactus abnormis 106, **127**, 161
Cactus cristates in cultivation............
...................................**10**, **139**, **141**
Cactus cristates in habitat 50, **51-62**
Caralluma **219**
    speciosa **219**
Carnegiea 111, 172
    gigantea ....
    ....**10**, **115**, 150, **177**, **178**, 279
Caryophyllales 64
Celosia **43**
Cephalocereus senilis **179**
Ceraria 147
Cereus 100, 107, 138, 143, 172
    'Abnormis' ....
    ....**106**, **107**, **127**, 146, 161, 279
    hildmannianus 45
        monstrosus **107**
        'Yellow Lion' 133
    jamacaru **55**
    peruvianus..............................45
        monstrosus 106, 279
    seedlings **107**

Cereus (contd.)
    spegazzinii **179**
    uruguayensis 45
    variabilis 'Monstrosus' **106**
    'Vortex' **116**, **140**
Ceropegia linearis 147
    linearis ssp. *woodii* 'Lady Heart' .....
    ....218, **223**
    stapeliiformis 218, **219**
Chahinian, J. 93-95, 139, 150, 251
Charles, Graham 50
Chiastophyllum oppositifolium **235**
Chim[a]era ....13, **67**, 82, 91 *et seq.*,
    ....**91-93**, 251
    creation **95-97**, **145**, 150
    cryptic 95
    mutilation 151
    origin 91, 95, 97
    tests for 151
    variegated 91-95
Chlorophyll 64, 75
Chloroplast 64
Chlorosis 74
    infectious 74-75
Christmas cactus See *Schlumbergera*
Christophe, Alain 225
Chromoplast 64
Cintia napina **105**
Cipocereus See *Pilosocereus*
Cleistocactus 148
    parapetiensis **20**
    ritteri **180**
    strausii **180**
    'Quantum Leap' **105**, **129**
Collections **10**, **13**, **83**, **139**,
    ....**141**, **163**, **179**, **203**, **207**,**208**
Colour ....64 *et seq.*
Compositae See Asteraceae
Compost See Soil
Conophytum 267
Copiapoa 116
    cinerea **11**, **57**, **118**
    columna-alba **57**
    haseltoniana **11**
    humilis **105**
    laui **145**
    marginata 140
    rupestris **57**
    tenuissima **17**, **181**
Cordyline 143, 251
Corynebacterium fascians 111
Coryphantha 172
    recurvata **180**
Cotyledon orbiculata **236**
    tomentosa 76
        'Cream Topping' **76**
        'White Palm' **236**
        'Yellow Palm' **76**, **236**
Crassula capitella 117, **119**
    conjuncta **236**
    muscosa **109**
        'Cristata' **109**, **169**, 235
        'Monstrosa' **109**, 235, **237**
    multicava 'Panache' **78**
        'Variegata' **77**, **78**
    orbicularis **24**, **118**, **119**
    ovata 121, 147, **238**
        'Gollum' ...121, **122**, 134, **237**
        'Hummel's Sunset' **238**
        'Obliqua Variegata' **238**
    rupestris 'Whiteout' **238**, 278
    sarmentosa 'Comet' 150, **239**, 278

Crassulaceae 172, 231-250
x *Cremneria expatriata* **155**
Cremnophila 155
Crest, Cristate, Cristation
  See Fasciation
Crown gall 110
Cryptanthus 251
Cryptomeria 138
Cultivar 139
Cultivation ....141 *et seq.*
  books on 142
  incorrect 151
  recommended plants 278-279

Dehn, R . N. 50
Delaetia 123
  woutersiana 123
Dichlamydeous chimera 92
Dichotomy 25, **26**, **27**
Dicotyledons, dicots 38, 39
  leaf variegation 75
Didiereaceae 273
Didymaotus lapidiformis **267**
Dioscorea 38
Diplocyatha See *Orbea*
Discocactus horstii 133, **181**
Disocactus 146
  x *mallisonii* **15**, **113**
Donaldson, Doug, Collection ...**179**, **203**
Dracaena 81, 143, 251
  draco 251, **255**
Dracaenaceae 251-255
Duvalia pillansii **220**

Echeveria 121, 146, 155, 235
  agavoides **240**
  coccinea 'Furry Fan' **155**
  crenulata **122**
  'Easter bonnet' 142
  elegans x *agavoides* **240**
  'Fantasia Carol' **240**
  gibbiflora 'Carunculata' **121**, **122**
  glauca **240**
  'Hoveyi' **103**
  pulvinata 'Frosty' **240**
    'Tricolor' **241**
  purpusorum **241**
  'Ramiletta' **31**
  setosa 40
    'Candy Floss' **31**, 278
  'Topsy Turvy' **103**, **137**
  'Zahnii' 103
Echinocactus grusonii **120**, **181**, **182**
  ingens **27**
  'Moelleri' 133
  texensis 133
Echinocereus **120**, **184**
  brandegeei **183**
  coccineus 120, **183**
  engelmannii 140
  'Fred' **109**
  knippelianus 105, **182**
  pulchellus **125**
  reichenbachii 27, **29**, 45
    meristem 25, **26**, **29**
  russanthus **183**
  scheeri 120
  viereckii 120
  viridiflorus **183**
Echinofossulocactus See *Stenocactus*
Echinopsis **37**, **64**, **96**, 97, 100, 109,
  ....**145**, 146, **149**, 172
  backebergii **156**
  chamaecereus 'Crassicaulis Cristata'
  ....**43**, **44**, 146, **184**, 279
    'Golden Peanut' **63**
    'Rainbow Fan' **134**

Echinopsis (contd.)
  densispina **90**, 123
  eyriesii **13**
    'Two-step Art' 133
  ferox **58**
  haematantha **32**, **33**, **58**
  'Haku Jo' 103, **104**
  'Johnson's Gold' **19**, 78, **80**
  lageniformis 'Jock, Dick & Willy'.......
  ....**109**, 279
  multiplex 103, 133, 147
  pachanoi 147
  rebutioides 123
  spachiana 147, 278
  'Stern von Lorsch' 123
  tubiflora 133
Endogenous origin 93, 97, **151**
Epicacti, epiphytes - rarity of teratology
 172
Epidermis 91
Epithelantha micromeris **28**, **53**, 97, 133
Eriospermum dregei **105**
Eriosyce **160**
  bulbocalyx **59**
  occulta **202**
  taltalensis 123
  umadeave **59**
Escobaria minima **113**
Espostoa ritteri **165**
Euphorbia 146, **204**
  abyssinica 143, 204
    'Milky Totem' **214**, 278
  x *bothae* 'Needle Hills' **168**
  bussei **204**, **205**
  cactus tortirama 116
  canariensis 147
  erythraeae 143
  flanaganii 143, **206**, **207**
  fruticosa **109**, 147, **207**
  groenewaldii 116, **117**
  gummifera **207**
  hallii **208**
  horrida **208**
  ingens 134
  lactea 134, 146, 204, 278
    'Spring Horse' 204, **207**, **209**
    'White (Grey) Ghost' ....
    ....204, **214**
  ledienii **204**
  mammillaris 147, **209**
  milii **210**
   'Golden Crown' **24**, **215**
  multiclava 27
  neriifolia **169**, **210**, **211**
    'Giraffe Horn' 134, **137**
  obesa ....
  ....147, **154**, **204**, **212**, **215**
    'Rocky Mountain' **211**, 279
  officinarum **205**
  piscidermis 27, **41**, **213**, 279
  ramiglans **212**
  resinifera **213**
  submammillaris 'Indian Corn' ....
  ....204, **214**, 278
  suzannae 78, **79**, 147, **204**
    'Maelstrom' ....
    ....78, 134, **137**, 204, **216**
  tirucalli 'Sticks of Fire' **87**
  tortirama **105**, 116
  trigona 'Red Ghost' 204, **214**
  turbiniformis **213**
  woodii 29, **30**, 143, **204**, **274**
    'Bighead Medusa' **30**, 275
    'Salad Bowl' **29**
Euphorbiaceae 204-217
Fasciation .... 9, 25 *et seq.*,**163**, 275
  definition 9, 32
  induced 40
  infective 41

Fasciation (contd.)
  inheritance 41-43
  initiation 41, 138
  occurrence in plants 38
  types of **26**, **32**
  in the wild 45, **46-62**
Faucaria **267**
  'Great Snow Stream' **269**
  'Star' **268**
  tuberculosa 121
x *Ferobergia* **124**
  'Gil Tegelberg' **124**
Ferocactus 124, 172
  echidne **202**
  glaucescens 133
  horridus **111**
  wislizeni
  ....**10**, **37**, 111, **114**, **184**, **185**
Flowers, double 13, **123**
  fasciated **33**
  variegated 74
Foliar follies 14
Frailea **17**
  castanea 133
Frithia **267**
Furcraea 251

x *Gasteraloe* 'Green Ice' **258**
Gasteria **22**, 256, **260**, **261**
  bicolor 'Golden Long Tongue' **259**
  carinata **259**
  disticha **259**
  'Double Carver' **123**
  gracilis **86**
  'Little Warty' **260**
  nitida 'Yellow Cow' **21**
  pillansii **260**
  'Royston's Fan' **261**
Gene, unstable 78
Geohintonia 172
  mexicana 133, **186**
Glossary 277
Glottiphyllum linguiforme
  'Yellow Tongue' 267, **269**
Graft hybrid 95
Grafting 80, 146-147, 150
  chimera production 95, **96**
  seedlings 147, 150
  test for pathogens 151
Graptopetalum **242**
Gymnocalycium **13**, 97, 172, 279
  anisitzii 133
  denudatum 97
  fleischerianum 133
  gibbosum 133
  hossei 133
  mihanovichii 65, **66-69**,
  ....**83**, 97,133, 146,
  ....**186**, 200, **202**, **203**
    'Hibotan' **67**, 97, 99, **135**
    'Hibotan Nishiki' **66**, **67**, **202**
    'Kimbotan' **67**
    'Pinkbotan' **67**
    'Ruby Ball' 97
    'Tegelberg's Beauty' **37**
  mostii 133
  mucidum **34**
  ochoterenae 133
  pflanzii 133
  quehlianum 133
  riojense **60**
  saglione **60**
  'New World Crown Brocade'.....133
  schickendantzii 133
  spegazzinii 133
Haageocereus pseudomelanostele ...**187**
  weberbaueri **187**
Hammer, Steven 267

Harrisia bonplandii 103, 147
   'Jusbertii' 103
Haworthia 81, 142, 256
   arachnoidea 256
   attenuata **85**
      'Golden Arrow' **262**
      'Little Lemon' **262**
      'Sparkler' **263**
      'White Arrow' **262**
   bolusii **263**
   chloracantha **263**
   cooperi **263**
   cuspidata **85**, **263**
   cymbiformis **23**
      'Chik-chun Mak' **170**
      'Harry Mak' 16, **23**, **263**
   fasciated **38**
   limifolia 'Stripes' **23**, **264**
   maughanii See truncata
   maxima **264**
   pygmaea **264**
      'Fan of Woodstock' **264**
   reinwardtii **264**
   rigida **264**
   subattenuata **265**
   truncata 16, **22**, 125, **266**
   turgida **266**
   viscosa **85**, **266**
Heidelberg University Botanic Gardens
....144, 273
Herdt, De, Nursery **163**
Higgins, Vera 41
Hirao, H. 97
Hirose & Yokoi
....75, 81, 172, 225, 251, 256, 267, 271
Hosta 81
Houghton, A.D. 7
Hoya 218
Huernia pillansii 41
   reticulata 39, **40**
Hunter, M. 204
Hybrid 124, 150
Hylocereus 97, 99
   undatus 97, 147
      'Pictus' **65**, 200
+ *Hylogymnocalycium* 'Singular'............
.....................97, **98-99**, **130**, **167**, 279

ICBN; International Code of
   Botanical Nomenclature 139
ICNCP; International Code of
   Nomenclature for Cultivated Plants
.................................139, 140, 161

Jatropha dioica 204
Johnson, Harry 139

Kalanchoe beharensis 121
   beharensis 'Fangs' 121
   blossfeldiana 278
      'Colour Spoon' **241**
      'Variegata' **242**
   fedtschenkoi 'Painted Butterfly' ..**242**
   manginii 'Golden Nodding' **242**
   'Pink Butterflies' **170**
Kleinia See *Senecio*

Larryleachia 218, 279
   cactiformis 45, **46**
   marlothii **46**
   perlata **221**
Leaves, abnormalities 14, **121-122**
   fasciated **36**
   variegation patterns **75**, **82**

Leuchtenbergia 124
   principis **113**
Lewisia cotyledon 271
Liana **274**
Lithops 267
   aucampiae 267
   bromfieldii 267
   fulviceps 267
   hookeri **270**
   lesliei 267
   pseudotruncatella **36**, 267
   'Steineckeana' 267
   vallis-mariae 267
Lobivia See *Echinopsis*
Lodoicea 37
Lophocereus See *Pachycereus*
Lophophora 172
   williamsii **18**, **54**, **88**

Mace, Tony 110
Machaerocereus See *Stenocereus*
Mak, Harry 134, 262
   collection **68-69**, **85**,
........................**163**, **262-266**
Mammillaria **13**, **15**, **89**, 172, 279
   bocasana 'Caterpincy' **105**
   'Fred' **105**, **108**, 109,
   ....**130**, **138**, **166**, 279
   'Multilanata Crest' **188**, 278
   carmenae **188**
   carnea **52**
   deherdtiana **149**
   duwei **188**
   elegans **188**
   elongata **11**, **189**, 278
   'Freaky' **105**, 279
   geminispina **42**
   gracilis 'Bunty' **20**, **135**
   grusonii **53**
   guelzowiana 123
   hahniana **189**
   hernandezii **153**
   heyderi **51**
   karwinskiana 110
   lasiacantha **189**
   longiflora **159**
   magnimamma 133
   marksiana **89**
   microcarpa 36
   muehlenpfordtii **27**
   nunezii **189**
   painteri **199**
   perbella **26**
   prolifera 140
   'Rocky Hill' **131**
   schiedeana var. plumosa **189**
   spinosissima **31**, **189**
   'Crested Pico' **191**
   'Swordfish' **105**
   supertexta **190**
   theresae **190**
   wildii **191**
   zeilmanniana **159**
Maranta **274**
Masters, M.T. 9, 105, 117
Matucana aurantiaca **61**
   elongata **62**
   formosa **61**
   haynei **62**
   madisoniorum **203**
Matuszewski, G. F. 50
Melocactus 16, **17**, 29
   broadwayi **35**
   intortus **6**
Mericlinal chimera **92**, 93, **95**
Meristem 25, **26**, 91, 94, 111
   elongated 31, 172

Micropetaly 123
Mikhaltsov, Anatoly 200, 201
Miller, Philip 63, 81, 142, 218
Mirabilis jalapa 78
Mixoploid 95
Monadenium ellenbeckii **216**
   lugardae **217**
Monanthes **231**
Monilaria moniliformis **21**, 267, **268**
Monochlamydeous chimera 92
Monocotyledons, monocots 38, 39
   leaf variegation **75**
Monstrosity, monstrose ....
...............9, 13, 105 *et seq.*, **127** *et seq.*
Monvillea See *Cereus*
Moran, Reid 46
Multiplex crest **26**, 27
Mutant, mutation 80, 91
Mycoplasma 111
Myrtillocactus **110**
   eichlamii **156**
   geometrizans 147, **165**

Names, naming 139-140
Neolloydia conoidea **51**
Neoporteria See *Eriosyce*
Nerium 147
Newton, Len **46**, **47**, **48**, 116, 272
Nolina 251
Nomenclature See Names
Notocactus See *Parodia*

Obregonia 172
   denegrii 133, **192**
Oenothera 32, 40
Opuntia **13**, 111, 146
   clavarioides 33, **34**, 218
   cylindrica **31**, 139
   erectoclada **193**
   ficus-indica 147
   'Eyeful'................**121**, 133, **136**
   'Reticulata'...........................**276**
   imbricata 146, 278
   lanceolata **193**
   mamillata **131**
   'Maverick' **112**, 279
   microdasys **112**, 151
   monacantha 147
   orbiculata 111
   ovata **112**
   ramosissima 45
   robusta 147
   tuna 'Monstrosa' 111
Orbea ciliata...33, **34**, **154**, 218, **221**, 279
   variegata 27, **29**, 218, **222**
Oreocereus 172
   celsianus **56**, **90**, **194**
Orostachys iwarenge 235
   'Fuji' **64**, **244**, 279
   'Phoenix' **244**
   spinosus 235, **243**
Oroya borchersii **62**
Othonna herrei 228
Oxalis peduncularis **270**

Pachycereus fulviceps **125**
   marginatus 140, **194**
   pringlei 110, **194**
   schottii 45, 107, **108**
   'Mieckleyanus' 108, 279
   'Monstrosus'
   ....**14**, **29**, 107, **108**, 279
Pachyphytum 235
   compactum 'Brainwave' **244**
Pachypodium 146

Pachypodium (contd.)
   geayi **224**
   horombense 224
   lamerei **15**, **25**, **28**, 40, **45**,
      74-75, 147, 150, **224**, **225**, **226**
      'Curlycrest' ....
      ....27, **28**, 31, 146, **225**, 279
      'Particolour' ....
      ....**12**, 78, 225, **227**, 279
   leaf grafts 151
   namaquanum ....
   ....45, 46, **47**, **224**, 225
   succulentum 224
x *Pachyveria* 235
Parodia **18**, 172
   buiningii **195**
   crassigibbus **118**
   leninghausii **195**
   magnifica **157**
   mammulosa **90**, 133
   'Mirabilis' **195**
   ottonis **131**
   scopa **195**
   werneri **157**
Passifloraceae 272
Pedilanthus macrocarpus 204, **217**
   tithymaloides 204, **217**
Peperomia magnoliifolia 'Green & Gold' ..
....143
Pereskia 172
Pereskiopsis 146, 147, 150, 172
   porteri 147
Periclinal chimera **92**, **93**, 95
Pests 145-146
Phalangial crest **26**, 27, **32**
Phoradendron diguetianum 110
Phormium 251
Pigments 64
   carotenoid 64
   cell sap 64
   plastid 64
Pilosocereus **148**
   azureus **19**
   bradei **196**
   gounellei **56**
   lanuginosus **196**
   pachycladus **19**
Plastid 64, 75
Pleiospilos 267
Portulaca 'Coral Ice' 271
   grandiflora **123**
Portulacaceae 271
Portulacaria **13**
   afra 147, **271**
Praeger, Lloyd 231
Proliferation ....**13**, 41, 111 *et seq.*
Propagation 146-147, 150
Pygmaeocereus bylesianus................**40**
Pyrrhocactus See *Eriosyce*

Rauh, Werner 204, 273
Rebutia 172
   canigueralii **19**, **158**, **196**
   einsteinii **158**
   heliosa **34**, **160**
   krainziana 'Haywire' **132**
      'Prodigy' **121**
   steinbachii 36, **197**
Reinelt, Frank 66
Reversion 39-40, **45**
Rhynchosia 274
Ring cristate **32-35**
Rohdea 81
Roots, fasciated **36**, **258**
Salm-Dyck, J. 65, 106, 200
Sansevieria ....
..................74, 143, 146, 251, 274, 279

Sansevieria (contd.)
   chimeras **93**, 94
   laurentii 161, 278
   mixoploid 95
   mutation pathways 150
   trifasciata 125, 143, 150, 251
      cultivars **93**, **94**, 95
      'Laurentii' 161
      'Moonshine' 146
      'Silver Hahnii' 146
Sarcocaulon peniculinum **105**
Schlumbergera 172
   x *buckleyi* **74**, **87**
x *Sclerinocereus* 'John White' ....
....**105**, **124**, 125
Sclerocactus mesae-verdae **132**
   papyracanthus **105**
Sectorial chimera **92**, **93**, **95**
Sedum **132**, 231
   acre 231
   album **245**
   erythrostictum 231, **245**
   kamtschaticum 231
   lineare 231
   lucidum **246**
   makinoi 231
   pachyphyllum 'Multifingers' ....
....**171**, **246**
   praealtum 'Jade Fan' **171**
   reflexum 231
   rubrotinctum 'Aurora' 103, **246**
   rupestre 231, **247**, 278
   sieboldii 'Mediovariegatum' ....
..............................**87**, 231, **247**, 278
   spurium 231
Seed raising 150, 151
Selenicereus spinulosus 147
Sempervivum 16, 231
   arachnoideum 231
   'Botterbun' **248**
   calcareum 'Grigg's Surprise' ......
....**21**, **102**
   ciliosum **248**
   'Fuzzy Wuzzy' **249**
   'Hungry Puppy' **249**
   montanum 231
   'Oddity' **102**
   tectorum 103
Senecio anteuphorbium **228**
   articulatus **228**
      'Candlelight' **64**, **228**
   ficoides 147, 229
   jacobsenii 228
   kleinia 228
      'Candystick' ....
...................................**13**, 80, **81**, 228, **229**
   mweroensis 228
   pendulus 228
   radicans 228
   rowleyanus 'String of Pearls' ....
....228, **230**, 278
   serpens 'Albert Baynes' ....
...........................27, **28**, 40, 228, **230**
   stapeliiformis 'Panoply' ....
....**167**, 228, **230**
Sequoia 138
Show, teratophytes exhibited **164**
Shurly, Ernest 172
Sinocrassula yunnanensis **168**, **250**
Smith, Mark 35
Soil preferences 144
Solenostemon 274
Somaclonal variation 138
Spinelessness 14, **15**, 120
Spiral torsion 14, 116-119
Sport See Mutant
Stapelia See also *Orbea*
   gigantea 147

Stapelianthus pilosus **222**
Stenocactus 172
   crispatus **153**
   phyllacanthus 45, **46**
   vaupelianus **197**
Stenocereus 111, 172
   eruca **198**
   griseus 172
   gummosus **49**, **62**
   thurberi **115**
Strawberry, fasciation in 43
Sulcorebutia See *Rebutia*

Talinum crassifolium 271
Taraxacum 40
Tavaresia 279
   barklyi **223**
Teratology 9, 14
Teratomania, quest for novelties ....
....150-151
Teratophile, teratophilia 14, 16
Teratophobe, teratophobia 14
Teratophyte 14
   appeal 161
   books on...................................**283**
   origin 9, 14
Tillandsia 251
Tomato, fasciation in 43
Toumeya See *Sclerocactus*
Tree, Bill & Yvonne 100
Trelease, W.A. 75, 76, 251
Trichocaulon See *Larryleachia*
Trichocereus See *Echinopsis*
Tumour **110**, 111
Turbinicarpus lophophoroides **149**
   pseudopectinatus **198**

+ *Uebelechinopsis* 100-101
   'Treetopper' **100-101**
Uebelmannia 172
   pectinifera 100, **199**
Unifacial fasciation **25**
Unilateral fasciation **25**

Variegation, variegates **8**, 9, **13**, 63
.................*et seq.*, 142, **164**, **203**, 275
   in cacti ....200 *et seq.*
   genetically controlled 75-76
   graft-transmitted 74
   induced 81
   inherited 81
   natural 74
   origin 80-83
   patterns **75**, 201
   reciprocal 76
   types of ....74 *et seq.*, 201
Virus 41, 74, 75
Vries, H. De 9

Watering 144-145
Weberbauerocereus See *Haageocereus*
Witches' broom 111
Wolthuys, J.J.v. 14, 138
Worsdell, W. C. 9, 105

Yucca 143, 251